HENRY HARRIS

MODEL SOLDIERS

OCTOPUS BOOKS

Acknowledgements

The author and publishers wish to thank the following owners and collectors for kind permission to reproduce their models and illustrations: HRH the Duke of Gloucester, figure 19; the Duke of Marlborough, figure 25; General Angenot, figures 34, 35, 52, 53, 64, 67; Colonel C. W. A. Bath, figures 88, 119; Peter Blum Esq., figures 61, 74; Monsieur Boverat, figure 23; Monsieur Broumes, figure 93; Y. M. Carmen Esq., figure 89; A. Cleaver Esq., figure 124; L. H. Cox Esq., figure 14; Captain R. S. Dilley, figures 1, 62, 94, 96, 97, 99, 100, 101, 102, 108, 127, 128, 131; Graham Farrish, figure 132; Russell Gammage, figures 60, 75, 81, 82, 90, 132; J. J. Garratt Esq., figures 2, 3, 4, 5, 6, 7, 8, 9, 18, 20, 22, 24, 26, 28, 55, 59, 68; I. N. Greene Esq., figure 107; Monsieur A. Gritton, figure 63; J. Gubbins Esq., figure 106; Colonel J. A. Jewson, figure 28; Madame Metayer, figure 57; Patrick Murray Esq., figures 17, 54; René North Esq., figures 16, 58, 123; Monsieur Soubeiran de Pierres, figures 10, 11; T. Sutton Esq., 68; Glenn Thompson Esq., 79, 80, 83.

The author and publishers are also grateful to the Commandant, Guards Depot, Pirbright, for kind permission to reproduce figure 42; to the Curator, Sherwood Foresters' Museum, Derby, for figure 15; to Bryan Latham Esq. and Messrs Alex Tiranti for figure 50, reproduced from *Victorian Staffordshire Pottery Figures*; and to the following museums British Museum, figures 3, 5, 7; Bayerisches Nationalmuseum, Munich, figures 22, 24; the Bodleian Library, Oxford, figure 6; Cairo Museum, figure 4; Imperial War Museum, London, figures 48, 49; Irish Military College Museum, The Curragh, figures 21, 56, 104, 120, 121; London Museum, Kensington Palace, figure 9; Ministry of Works, figure 20 (Crown Copyright reserved); Museum of Childhood, Edinburgh, figures 32, 51, 54; National Army Museum, Sandhurst, figures 12, 13, 36, 37, 40, 41, 43, 45; Naval Museum, Madrid, figures 75, 84; New York Military Historical Society, figures 61, 74; North Staffordshire Regimental Museum, Lichfield, figures 46, 47; Royal Army Service Corps Museum, Aldershot, figures 44, 98; Royal Scots Museum, Edinburgh, figure 39; US Marine Corps Museum, Quantico, Virginia, figures 72, 77, 78; US Marine Corps Memorial Museum, Philadelphia, figure 71; US Military Academy, West Point, 69, 70; US Naval Museum, Annapolis, 73.

The author and publishers are also obliged to the following commercial makers for permission to reproduce their models: W. Britain Ltd., figure 31; Mignot, figure 27; Norman Newton Ltd., 65, 76; Messrs Staar, 55; Messrs Airfix, 11, 112, 113. Figures 10, 11, 23, 27, 34, 35, 52, 53, 63, 64, 67, 93 were photographed by E. Boudot Lamotte, Paris; the endpapers and figure 103 by H. Tempest Ltd., Cardiff; and figure 19 by the Camera Press (Tom Blau). Figures 61, 74 are by Peter Blum; figures 16, 58, 123 by René North; and figure 84 by W. Britain Ltd. Figures 26, 92 are by Messrs A. C. Cooper; figures 85, 96 by Federico Arborio Mella; figures 17, 32, 39, 51, 54, 91 by Tom Scott, Edinburgh; figure 15 by Winter, Derby; figures 21, 56, 104 by T. Gunn; Dublin; figures 79, 80, 83, 106, 107 by J. D. Barry, Dublin; figure 14 by F. G. Rottner, Brighton. Figures 69, 70 were provided by the US Military Academy, West Point; figure 71 by the US Marine Corps Memorial Museum, Philadelphia; figures 72, 77, 78 by the US Marine Corps Museum, Quantico; and figure 73 by the US Naval Adademy, Annapolis. Figures 3, 5, 7 are by the British Museum and figure 6 by the Bodleian Library; 130 from Capt B. H. Liddell Hart. All the other photographs were specially taken for this book by Alan Meek from the collections mentioned above and from the author's collection.

This edition first published 1972 by
OCTOPUS BOOKS LIMITED
59 Grosvenor Street, London W.1

ISBN 7064 0042 9

Preceding page
Royal carriages in a courtyard, including the Coronation coach on the right

PRODUCED BY MANDARIN PUBLISHERS LIMITED AND PRINTED IN HONG KONG

Contents

Models and their Collectors

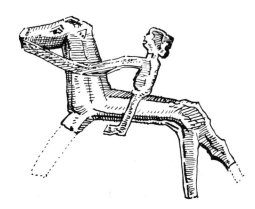

2 Early model soldiers were either votive offerings or grave-furniture. This bronze figure is from Rosegg, Carinthia, c. 1000 BC

ALTHOUGH THE GROWTH of societies devoted to the study and collection of little warriors is a twentieth-century development, the fascination for man of miniature models of soldiers and their impedimenta has existed for several thousand years. Museums in many parts of the world include among their treasures examples of small martial 'figurines', dating almost from the beginning of time to modern works of craftsmanship and art. Made from wood, clay, base or precious metal, as well as more transient materials, they were intended to portray a side of life as old as man himself. The collector of today is found in many countries and walks of life. It was estimated a few years ago that throughout the world there were over a hundred thousand serious collectors of model soldiers, and an American society which recently conducted a survey of vocations among its members discovered that they ranged over fifty-seven professions and employments, from student to salesman, artist to attorney, and psychiatrist to postman. Recent research has brought to light previously little-known references to the part which model soldiers have played in the lives of great men, as well as clues to the purpose for which the prehistoric figures were made.

The earliest known models are classed by archaeologists as tomb furniture, a category which includes many small ancient works of art [figure 2]. Many must be of votive origin, but some at least were playthings. In fact J. G. Garratt, the author of *Model Soldiers: A Collectors' Guide* (the standard work on the subject), believes that many served a dual purpose like the doll, which as Anatole France has said, 'is like the lesser idol of antiquity'. As the doll was to the girl, so was the toy soldier to the boy.

In Europe there have been finds of a similar nature. From Rosegg in Carinthia a grave tumulus yielded a number of crude horsemen [figure 2] which Ebert in his *Reallexicon der Vorgeschichte* declared to be from the Hallstatt

1 (*left*) George Washington, a casting by Winkler from a master mould by Eriksson, in the collection of Captain Dilley

5

3 Toy figure of a Roman soldier in flat, moulded lead, of the third century AD

4 The earliest model soldiers in existence: Egyptian troops of painted wood from the tomb of Masashite, 11th dynasty

period (1000 BC). A more elaborate find from the same period and area is the 'Strettweg Cart', a flat vehicle on four wheels bearing a female figure and escorted by four horsemen five inches high. The lands and islands of the Mediterranean have all provided evidence of the ancient making of model warriors in metal or clay, and a particularly noble example is a Greek equestrian figure in bronze fourteen and a half inches high [figure 5]. Several Classical writers mention a 'Troy Game', in which a little horse containing warriors was used. The Romans produced small warlike figures, which have been found in Spain, Germany, Britain and as far away as Abyssinia [figure 3]. Some of these were votive figures, but others may well have been children's playthings.

In common with most of the arts there is a gap in the Dark Ages, but with the reconstruction of society and the spread of learning, interesting references to military models have been preserved from the Middle Ages onwards. These include figures which may have been pilgrims' badges or Crusaders' talismans; their chief interest to the collector lies in their design and method of production. They were made of flat tin, anticipating the commercial era of the tin soldier six to seven centuries later. Such mediaeval models include a Thomas-à-Becket in the British Museum, a knight in the Cluny Museum, Paris, and the group of knights at a tourney, found at Magdeburg in 1956.

Naturally they were crude in outline and detail compared to modern equivalents, but they reveal an interest in models as a method of recording history.

That playing with three-dimensional or 'round' models of a military nature was a favourite game in the Middle Ages is revealed by illustrations in manuscripts, of which the

5 A bronze model, 14½ inches high, of an equestrian warrior from archaic Greece

best known are the *Hortus Deliciarum*, by the Abbess Herrad of Landsberg, and another (illustrated in Beard's *Miniature Armours*) in the Bodleian Library. The sons of princes and nobles staged model tournaments, using miniature knights which by an ingenious mechanism of wheels and strings charged each other in a realistic manner, splintering their lances, obligingly made of brittle wood for this purpose. In the *Weisskönig* of Hans Burghmaier there is a woodcut showing a young prince, later the Emperor Maximilian I, at a game of model jousting with a playmate [figures 6, 7]. Examples of this kind of model are to be seen in Paris and in the Bayerisches Museum in Munich. The wooden horses are some eight inches tall and eleven inches long on four wheels, and have tails of natural horse-

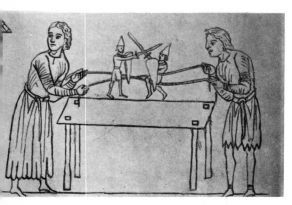

6 In the Middle Ages games were played with hand-manipulated toy soldiers. An illustration from the *Hortus Deliciarum*

7 A woodcut by Burghmaier, c. 1516, shows the use of model knights in a tournament game

hair. They are ridden by jointed dolls encased in miniature armour, accurate in the smallest details. From the similarity of these two models J. G. Garratt assumes that they originally formed a pair, emanating from the same workshop, and that they represent a Christian knight and an infidel. He dates them about 1550. A group of tournament toys cast in bronze (the horses hollow cast), dating from about 1490, were shown at an exhibition of armour in the Tower of London in 1949. They are now on show in the Kunsthistorisches Museum in Vienna. Modern collectors, who are inclined to take offence when their collections are referred to as toys, may derive some consolation in learning that in the seventeenth and eighteenth centuries the word 'toy' was an expression used in the craft guilds to describe any small model of a larger piece. Such miniatures would be of the finest workmanship, as they were often made for the great to give as gifts to their friends.

Among the models made of precious metals by craftsmen of the period are the nefs or table-ships preserved in the Cluny and the Victoria and Albert Museums. The former shows the Emperor Charles V surrounded by courtiers, musicians, soldiers and sailors, some of which moved about the deck. The ship itself is gold and silver, and the figures are of gilded and enamelled bronze. The nef in the Victoria and Albert Museum in London forms part of the Rothschild Collection and is manned by tiny soldiers and sailors. Both of these models are of German origin. Clocks have, somewhat naturally, also featured in the products of model soldier craftsmen, and one notable example now in the British Museum was also contrived as a nef, and is believed to have been made for the Emperor Rudolph II. When European troops entered the Winter Palace in Peking at the time of the Boxer rising in 1900, a remarkable clockwork toy was retrieved from the debris. Constructed about 1750, of gilt and base metal, it is believed to have been made for the delight of the Emperor K'ien Lung; it is now known as 'King Edward VII's clock', because it was presented to the then Prince of Wales after the Boxer rising [figure 9].

'Put me and my army,' said General Wolfe in 1759, 'on the heights of Abraham, and French America is ours.' To overcome Montcalme's unassailable position the Navy rowed Wolfe's men to the foot of the cliffs at night, and helped them carry their guns and munitions to the top. This deed was later commemorated by a number of wood models of the ship's boats, filled with soldiers made of cork, and all

8 Mediaeval figures are widely collected, and they appeal particularly to students of heraldry. These 'Knights of Agincourt', brilliantly painted by J. J. Garratt, are Britain's models, apart from the figure with a pole-axe, which is a Starlux plastic

9 A clock of gilt metal made about 1750 for the Emperor K'ien Lung of China, presented to King Edward VII in 1900. The figures of painted tin revolved by clock-work

are painted in their correct colours. One is in the Castle Museum, York, another in the National Army Museum, Sandhurst, and others in the National Maritime Museum, Greenwich [figure 12].

Mention has already been made of the tournament toys of the young Prince Maximilian; many other royalty since have had the models of their day either as toys or for instruction or a mixture of both. Garratt tells us that 'early in the seventeenth century the Armoury of St James's Palace housed a great collection of models exhibiting every aspect of military life and every engine of land warfare known at the time'. They were apparently collected for the instruction of Henry, Prince of Wales, who died in 1612.

The Journal of a Doctor, Jean Heroard, who was a member of his court, tells of the playthings of the Dauphin, later Louis XIII. He possessed a silver ship, and later his mother, Marie de Medici, gave him a miniature army of three hundred silver soldiers made by one Nicolas Roger. (By a royal oversight, Roger was not paid and it was left to the Dauphin to settle for these when he became king). This Dauphin also cast his own soldiers '7 cm high, without

stands, pegged so as to fit into a board for arranging in battalions', as well as cannon 'which fired without bursting', a remark which reminds us of the hazards of early real-life gunnery when the 'pieces' were as dangerous to the men who fired them as to those at whom they were aimed. Louis XIV as Dauphin inherited this model army and reinforced it in 1650 by further troops also in silver, *'toute la cavalerie, infantrie et les machines de guerre'*, costing five thousand écus. This, in turn, was bequeathed to his eldest son, whose military education was supervised by Colbert. It was brought soldiers. They were returned to the Imperial Family at the time of the Second Empire and after a further alteration, in which the French Eagle and the numeral 22e were restored, became the playthings of the Prince Imperial. In 1870 they were given to the de Pierres family by the Empress Eugénie who orally testified as to their origin. They have remained in the proud possession of the de Pierres to this day [figures 10 and 11].

The now famous firm of Mignot was commissioned by Napoleon III to make a large solid lead collection for the Prince Imperial. These were brought by the family when they went into exile in England. The Prince was killed whilst serving with the British Army in Zululand in 1879, but the Empress Eugénie retained the models for a long time, giving some away to collectors and the remainder to the Duke of Alba in 1910. Napoleon III also had a collection of seventy-five soldiers in contemporary uniforms made of plaster of paris; finished with scrupulous care in every detail and supervised by the Emperor himself, they were displayed in the Tuileries. They were destroyed at the time of the Commune.

10, 11 (*above* and *below*) Among the most famous of all model soldiers are those made for the King of Rome, Napoleon's son, by the Goldsmith J. B. Odiot in 1812. They could be mounted by pins on a machine which moved the models in drill formations. The Colonel, made to represent the King of Rome, is in the centre foreground. Collection Soubeiran de Pierres

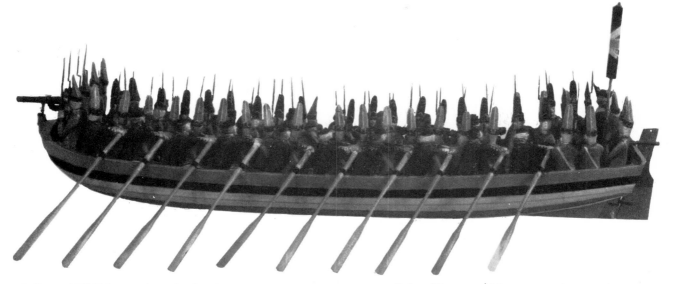

12 General Wolfe's assault on Quebec in 1759 was commemorated by a number of models. This example shows troops of painted cork, with weapons of metal, embarked in a wooden boat eighteen inches long. The regiment is not identified

13 A small wooden model of an officer, in the Coldstream Guards, carved by Richard Meadows while a prisoner-of-war at Lille in 1798. Now in the National Army Museum, Sandhurst

up to a new strength by 'figures of horses and men and pieces of artillery (and other bibelots)... produced by the most illustrious makers of Augsburg and Nuremberg...'.

These royal models were developed further by the great French military engineer Sebastian le Prestre de Vauban. This organisational genius and master of applied mathematics, a member of the *Académie des Sciences*, supervised a mechanism whereby the pieces '... went through the usual manoeuvres very ably; they marched... doubled their ranks, lowered their weapons, struck fire, shot off and retreated. Then the pikemen tried to knock the cavalrymen out of the saddles but these were quite prepared to defend themselves by firing their pistols.' Sad to say, this elaborate army on which so much inventive genius was expended is no more. Neither it, nor a cardboard one, *'une armée de XX escardines de Cavalerie Sa Majesté a commandé'*, has been preserved. Garratt concludes, rightly, I feel, that the silver was melted down to produce money for the more sanguinary wars of real life and the *Armée de Carte* met a more natural fate, although it has been said that a set preserved in the Invalides may be this one. The authorities of the Musée de l'Armée, however, do not think this likely. In this sphere, as in others, *Le Roi Soleil* had his imitators. In the 1670's the Prince Elector of Bavaria had a collection of models, including artillery, in the traditional German wood carving, a medium which enabled models to be available to rich and poor alike.

Preserved in France and on show to the public in 1960, is a remarkable set of models, the soldiers of the King of Rome. Originally made entirely of gold, they were the work of J. B. Claude Odiot, the Emperor's goldsmith, and are high-

14 A bivouac during the American War of Independence, modelled *c.* 1870 by Heyde of Dresden, a famous German maker of solid figures. He was the first manufacturer to construct figures in a great variety of postures and to sell boxed sets of assorted figures. Those shown here are 40 mm solids, in the collection of L. H. Cox

15 A ram has been the mascot of the Sherwood Foresters ever since the Indian Mutiny, when the original ram was rescued and awarded the Mutiny Medal

ly worked and engraved. The hundred and seventeen pieces represented the 22e Light Artillery, a traditional regiment of Corsica, and were a present to the little King from his Imperial parents in 1812. In 1814 the display was rescued by Queen Hortense and in 1822 was returned to the little exile after some alterations to make them resemble Austrian

Catherine the Great in her memoirs told of Tsar Peter III who, when Grand Duke, 'had an enormous number of model soldiers made of wood, lead, starch and wax arrayed on narrow tables occupying a whole room. He had strips of wire across the tables with strings attached. When the strings were pulled, the strips of wire made (according to him) sounds like the rolling fire of guns.' He celebrated all Court holidays regularly and every day there was a 'Guard Changing'. He himself attended this ceremony in uniform and those who were admitted to see these exercises were obliged to dress in the same way.

Among later sovereigns who were model soldier enthusiasts, Tsar Nicholas I owned a complete collection of Russian Guards regiments made by the German toy firm of Heinrichsen. In the conventional flat style, but slightly oversize, the firm gave them their special attention to ensure

16 A painted plywood cut-out of Robert Devereux, Earl of Essex, Master General of the Ordnance, 1597. A 1/16th scale model by R. North

17 Porcelain manufacturers in the eighteenth century, such as Worcester, Dresden and Meissen, made a number of military figures. A statuette of a drummer by Meissen, c. 1750-60, in the collection of Patrick Murray

18 The earliest mass-produced models were German flat figures made by J. G. Hilpert of Nuremberg in 1775. This is his model of Frederick the Great, based on a portrait by Chodowiecki, signed and dated 1777

19 Toy soldiers continue as popular playthings: Prince William of Gloucester with his models, photographed in 1956

their perfection and artistry. King Alphonso XIII of Spain, too, was a patron of the miniature soldier and intensely interested in the 'war game'. He combined with Kaiser Wilhelm II to present to the Tsar in 1910 a collection of over twenty thousand figures, eight inches high. Like much else, these disappeared in the Revolution. In nineteenth-century Germany, notable royal collectors included the King of Hanover, from whose collection ten figures are preserved in the Schloss Gmunden. Up to the Second World War the Hohenzollern Museum in Berlin held a collection of one hundred and forty figures representing Prussian regiments, the property of King Frederick William III, but unfortunately their present whereabouts is unknown.

Metals and cardboard, however, were not the only media in the construction of figures; the Gingerbread man had his military cousin, the gum-tragacanth, a sugar and flour figure which was hardened in a mould and then painted. These edible military figures were produced all over the Continent in the last three centuries and examples of them are preserved in the Kulmbach Museum. Peter III of Russia is said to have been particularly devoted to them and once ordered a rat which had eaten two to be sentenced to death by court martial. Whilst, strictly speaking, they are *objets d'art*, reference must also be made to the military figures

20 Part of the second Waterloo model by Captain Siborne showing the action of the British heavy cavalry around La Haye Sainte. This famous model is now in the Tower of London. Dated *c.* 1844

made in precious stones by Carl Peter Fabergé. In the Royal Collection at Sandringham there is, among many other figures, a marvellous five-inch high model of a Chelsea Pensioner. An Imperial German Horse Guard standing six inches high has a greatcoat of obsidian and a Russian Infantryman made for Grand Duke Nicolai Nicolaivitch is of nephrite and black jasper, the hand and face in orletz, eyes of sapphire and rifle and accoutrements of gold and silver. A Cossack commissioned by Czar Nicholas II has an overcoat of green jasper and gold, belt of porphyrite, face and hands of cachalong (an opaque type of opal), and hair and beard of grey jasper and eyes of gold.

The Battle of Waterloo is rightly regarded as one of the decisive battles of the world. It ended in the overthrow of the greatest military power in the world after twenty-three years of continuous fighting, and settled the affairs of Europe for a century. For the British Army it was the first

15

21 The Irish Brigade in the service of France, *c.* 1750. The standard-bearer and drummer of the Dillon Regiment are castings by Eriksson, the mounted figures of Fitz James's Regiment are by Winkler and the officer by Carmen. The latter is Colonel Hennessy, founder of the famous brandy firm

battle for which a medal was struck for all ranks, and everyone present had two years added to his service for all purposes. It is fitting therefore that England should have what must be the largest and most important collection of model soldiers made before the coming of mass production: the two Siborne layouts of the Battle of Waterloo.

Some time after the battle, Captain William Siborne, late 9th Foot, was commissioned by the Commander-in-Chief to supervise the making of a model of the Field of Waterloo. He spent several months on the field measuring and checking, and wrote innumerable letters to those who had taken part. Being refused the bulk of the money promised to finance the work, he completed it in 1838 at his own expense at a cost of three thousand pounds (raising a private loan to do so). The model was displayed at various places and now stands in the Royal United Services Institution in Whitehall, London. On a scale nine feet to one mile, it is some eighteen feet square and contains approximately a hundred and ninety thousand half-inch figures. Individually, they are indistinguishable, but an unforgettable impression is caused by their very mass.

In order to illustrate the battle in still greater detail, Siborne began a series of models on a larger scale, of which only one was completed (in 1844), the Charge of the British Heavy Cavalry around La Haye Sainte. It comprises some three thousand perfectly detailed figures, every one with moveable arms, the cuirassiers with tiny brass breastplates and the generals with removeable hats. After lying neglected in a warehouse in Ireland for over sixty years it was sent to the Staff College at Camberley. In 1935 Mr Charles Ffoulkes, the Master of the Armouries, arranged for it to be transferred to the Tower of London where it can be seen today. It was carefully restored by Mr H. Cawood to its present condition [figure 20].

It might be suspected that this stupendous quantity of models (nearly two hundred thousand, plus a great deal of scenery) was beyond the scope of one man to make in the period. J. G. Garratt, from whose researches the above information is drawn, has carefully investigated this aspect in Siborne's correspondence in the British Museum and official records of the War Office, and in the House of Commons Library. He could find no reference to any other makers or payments to anyone for such work; whether or not all the work was done by Siborne himself, it still remains a truly astonishing achievement for which his memory deserves to be kept alive by all collectors.

THE MASTER MODELLERS OF NUREMBERG - The army of Frederick the Great has been brilliantly described in other books, its drill, its training and its tactics. Brought to perfection, the infantry could shoot three times as fast as any other. Frederick's tactics (he introduced a new movement to the battlefield, the oblique order of attack) depended on performing a complex set of physical motions more efficiently than any of his enemies. The achievements of Frederick's armies led to the production of model soldiers on a scale never known before and in a fashion which is always to be associated with Germany, that of the flat figure.

It was begun about 1775 in Nuremberg by Johann Gottfried Hilpert with forty types of models of Frederican soldiers probably in tin, two to three inches high; and was continued by other makers in that town (Besold, Haffner, Stahl Gottschalk and Ammon). In Fürth in the 1790's there were eight model foundries, and there were others in Berlin, Luneberg and Württenberg by the turn of the century

22 German flats by Heinrichsen of Nuremberg c. 1870, who standardised the size of his figures to 30 mms, known as the 'Nuremberg scale' since 1848

23 The British as seen by the French. *Le Retour du parachutiste, 1944.* Collection M. Boverat

[figure 18]. The Nuremberg makers set a lasting fashion in style as well as material; the earliest figures were made of pure tin or a pewter mixture which permitted great detail in engraving. But these *zinnsoldaten* were soon diluted by various alloys although the original description has persisted to this day. Great artistry was shown by the engravers and designers who were either heads of the firms or master craftsmen, or were employed by small firms in what we today would call a 'consultancy' role. Designs ranged from Germans to Cossacks, and later British, French, Turks and Austrians, as well as every type of civilian activity then known, hunting, dancing, country life, social activities and folklore. In the nineteenth century civil and industrial developments were reflected by the output of the industry, the various wars providing a valuable stimulus, victors and vanquished being produced with impartiality.

The makers themselves had varying fortunes, Hilpert's pre-eminence being overtaken by Heinrichsen. Starting in Nuremberg in 1839 the original founder gained a gold medal for his engraving three years later. Beginning with Prussian Guards, Bavarian infantry and French lancers, the firm progressed through the years with Crimean, Russo-Turkish, Russo-Japanese, Boer War and Indian Mutiny figures. In 1848 Heinrichsen I began to standardise the size of his products to the 30 mm scale, which became known as the Nuremberg size, although not all the other manufacturers fell into line [figure 22].

After the First World War, Heinrichsen III made figures of that grim struggle, flame throwers, gas-masked troops and the impedimenta of trench warfare. In the great exhibition at Leipzig in 1930 most of the hundred dioramas were composed of Heinrichsen figures, Goths, Vikings, Knights and Red Indians as well as the other military figures. The firm is believed to have closed in 1945, and stocks taken over, but the widow lives and very occasionally supplies some favoured customer. Other contemporaries of Heinrichsen included Allgeyer of Fürth who produced excellent work, Denecke of Brunswick, Weygang of Göttingen and Haffner of Fürth, examples of whose work are now scarce. In Berlin two firms, Haselbach and Söhlke, made wide ranges of good popular models for many years, and in Hanover. Rieche produced from 1806 to 1945 a wide and interesting series of figures, until the moulds were taken over.

Flat figures dominated the German scene until the 1870's when as a result of French influence they began to evolve

24 Around 1870 German manufacturers began to turn from flat to solid figures. These solid lead polychrome figures were made by Haffner of Fürth *c.* 1867-86, who originally was a manufacturer of flats

to the semi-flat (or semi-round), but still solid. Haffner and Allgeyer (who exported much to France) and Söhlke led the field. Examples of these figures can be seen in the dioramas at Compiègne, in which twelve thousand pieces are assembled. Haffner then went completely 'solid' and models in the Bayerisches Museum at Munich are examples of very fine work in this style [figure 24].

But the name best known for German solid figures is that of Heyde of Dresden. Believed to have begun production in 1870, in seventy years the firm's output was prolific and was exported all over the world. Their popularity was due to the great variety of postures and types, and the grouping of assortments in boxed sets. Heyde's 'standard' size was 6 cm for a dismounted figure, with others to scale, although there were ranges in 40 mm and 7.75 cm. Heads were plugged, mounted men detachable from their steeds and there were many accessories [figure 32]. Although the range was wide (from Greeks and Trojans to the Imperial Durbar of 1910), Heyde's models were not very popular in Germany, and collectors can often validly criticise their bad anatomy, poor design and lack of animation. When Britain's hollow cast products began to rival them, Heyde produced models of the same type, described in his catalogue as 'soldiers made in the English way'. In the latter days of the German toy soldier market there were innumerable small makers and many of Heyde's designs were pirated (a practice not confined to that country) so that identification in many cases is difficult. Today Heyde is no more. In the air-raids of the

25 One of the earliest and finest of French model makers was Lucotte, who stamped his work with the Imperial bee. His figures of the Grande Armée are preserved at Blenheim Palace, where the mirrored case appears to double the numbers

Second World War the factory was destroyed.

Papier mâché was used for making soldiers in Germany at the end of the seventeenth century and two hundred years later in France, the figures being larger than the normal toy soldier. A model of Gulliver tied down by the Lilliputians, exhibited at the Great Exhibition of 1851 in London, was entirely made of *papier mâché*, including the minute soldiers. With the aim of making figures of a less destructible material than lead, a composition described as *carton comprimé* was used in France for a period, in the mid-nineteenth century. A diorama of the Crimean War had figures of this substance. German figures of composition material were made by 'Elastolin' throughout the last century

26 Kettle-drum carriage of the Master-General of the Ordnance of the British Army, *c.* 1720, which was drawn ahead of the artillery in the field. The carriage and drums are of carved wood, the men and horses are Britain's conversions. Author's collection

and up to the Second World War, when the factory was destroyed by bombing. It has since been rebuilt, and production of Wild West subjects is being followed by soldiers, but the material now used is more in the nature of a plastic and the figures are of greatly improved design. Another post-war German firm producing composition toys have revealed that they consist of kaolin, wood, flour, dextrin, casein, bone glue and water. Plaster of paris has also been used for figures, not, as might be expected, in the making of mould figures, but also for the finished work, especially for dioramas. Metallised compositions are a recent development, and aluminium has also been used for toy soldiers because it is durable, but the failure to achieve detail in casting makes it of little interest to collectors.

SOLDIERS OF FRANCE - 'You cannot beat the Maison du Roy', said the Duke of Marlborough. 'You have to destroy it.' This was accomplished only by the French themselves in the Revolution of 1789-92, and whilst the new Assembly was laying the foundations of what was to become the fabulous Imperial Guard, a man called Lucotte began to produce solid model soldiers or *figurines ronde-bosse*.

Little is known of Lucotte; his figures can be identified by the letters 'LC' stamped on the bases accompanied by the Napoleonic Imperial Bee, but exactly where he operated and when is to some extent a mystery. It is generally believed that at some date early in the nineteenth century he was bought up by Mignot, but this firm appears to be unable to confirm this. Garratt, who made persistent attempts to find out, states that Lucotte's mark was first used by the latter firm about 1825 which suggests incorporation about this time. Fortunately, Lucotte's work, which is of beautiful

27 '*Le Fleur au Fusil*', a graphic French representation of the opening of the First World War. The figures are of flat metal made by the French firm of Mignot, now the oldest toy-soldier firm in the world

28 (*below*) in 1893 William Britain of North London produced the first English hollow-cast models. These mounted figures of a Life Guards officer and trooper were the first Britain ever made

quality, has been preserved in several places. At Blenheim Palace, near Oxford, there is a collection of some three hundred and seventy models on view to the public. They make an impressive sight in mass and were presented to the present Marquis of Blandford by Major Paul Maze [figure 27].

To return to Mignot: having been reorganised several times and outstripped their competitors, this famous firm survives today in Paris, weathering the storms of some hundred and seventy years. They are now the oldest toy-soldier firm in the world. They have naturally specialised in French troops, particularly Revolutionary and First Empire, but in their latest catalogue there is a section headed 'From Antiquity to the First Empire', which includes Greeks, Romans, Crusaders and Mediaeval figures. Among models of many lands, is a very interesting range of historical figures including Cleopatra, Vercingetorix, Columbus, Washington, Queen Victoria, Lincoln and Pope Pius XV. It was estimated a few years ago that the firm had a hundred and fifty thousand moulds and they are constantly adding to their range [figure 27].

SOLDIERS OF THE QUEEN - Up to 1893, Great Britain, whose soldiers had by then carried her flag to every part of the world, looked to Germany for miniature reproductions of them: Allgeyer, Heinrichsen and later Heyde supplying a wide and plentiful variety. In that year the aptly named William Britain of North London produced a revolutionary

29 A 54 mm model of a Pioneer from the Fort Henry Guards of Canada, made by the famous English firm of Britain's. A fine example of a commercial product in the Author's collection

design of a solid (that is 'all round') soldier, the hollow-cast figure which was to make the firm an honoured name in the toy trade and by the 1950's the largest toy-soldier makers in the world. W. Britain had already been in the toy making business for fifty years and was famous for his mechanical toys and fund-raising novelties for charities. He had an inventive mind and his new technique of hollow casting by using less metal enabled him to produce soldiers cheaper than the German imports. His other great contribution was standardisation of size which enabled collectors to amass small armies and ushered in the era of nursery floor warfare.

Previously the great English nursery game had been toy trains, and Britain related the size of his soldiers to the then fashionable No 1 gauge of model railways [figure 30]. Natural conservatism towards all new things held up the venture until Britain induced a famous London store to open up a whole department with his new lines and 'Britains' achieved a break-through. From twenty varieties in 1895, production rose to five million castings in over a hundred varieties in 1905 (a gilt model of King Edward VII selling one million copies alone). In 1914 they were exporting to Germany as well as to other parts of the world. An insistence on accuracy (within economic limits) was also another element of Britain's success. He knew better than Heyde not to commit the unforgivable blunder of mounting Household Cavalry on brown horses. In 1905 the firm supplied a complete set of all their varieties, 'in correct uniforms even down to the stripes', to the Duke of York's School, and there was 'an extraordinary order from a former Secretary of State for War for a large set of soldiers'.

As real warfare was not quite 'total' during 1914-18, production continued at a reduced scale and it was in this period that my collection began. On his return from France in 1916, my father brought (as part of the gifts of a returning warrior) a selection of the famous red boxes. From this beginning and what I saw in shop windows, I caught the fever. When we were living in quarters at Aldershot, my weekly good-conduct reward was a box of Britains. My father, a professional soldier, was careful to keep a balance between the various arms and services, although I realise now that there was a bias towards his own cavalry regiment.

By 1918 my army was possibly 400-500 strong, and was paraded on a very large shelf. When I had laid it out, it would be inspected by our soldier servant. Towards the end of the War, I was taken to Dublin by my mother, my soldiers occupying a substantial part of our luggage. There I met another boy with a collection and we indulged in a crude form of war game, in which I lost many irreplaceable models. Some of my casualties were replaced by purchases from the Dublin shops. Although this was the time when anti-British feeling ran high in some quarters in Ireland, the red coat and horse and foot of Britain's army filled many shop windows.

In the general revulsion against war that came in the 1920's, toy soldiers lost much of their popularity, and Britain's was among the firms that turned their swords into ploughshares. Instead of soldiers they produced a farm series on the same scale, of animals, workers, vehicles and other items of the countryside, which in turn became just as popular. The hunt, the zoo and the circus series followed. When that exquisite piece of work, the Queen's Dolls House, was ordered by her late Majesty Queen Mary, the firm had the privilege of supplying some specially made 'toys', including two tiny boxes of minute soldiers. Rearmament and air-raid precaution in the late 1930's were reflected in the range; anti-aircraft guns, searchlights, barrage balloons and military vehicles appeared alongside new men, as well as the ever popular varieties of Guards and Highlanders which were especially popular abroad. At the beginning of the Second World War the firm was enjoined by the Government to continue making toy soldiers for export to America. This unusual way of earning dollars in wartime continued until a Congressman produced a toy Grenadier Guardsman in a debate on Lend Lease as an example of British war effort. To avoid further misunderstandings, the firm switched to more deadly production.

When toy production was resumed again, the Government ruled that every model should be exported because lead was too valuable for the home market. After 1947 some familiar

30 Examples of conversions by the Author from an unpainted standard Britain's figure (*centre*). Left, a District Commissioner of the British Colonial Service; right, a British general, undress uniform

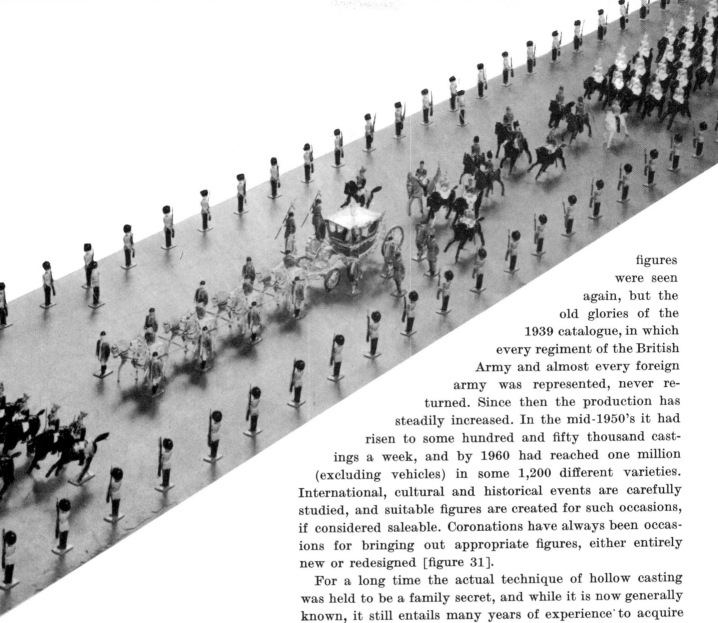

31 The Coronation procession of HM Queen Elizabeth II in 1953, an example of Messrs Britain's commercially painted figures, which are prized by many enthusiasts

figures were seen again, but the old glories of the 1939 catalogue, in which every regiment of the British Army and almost every foreign army was represented, never returned. Since then the production has steadily increased. In the mid-1950's it had risen to some hundred and fifty thousand castings a week, and by 1960 had reached one million (excluding vehicles) in some 1,200 different varieties. International, cultural and historical events are carefully studied, and suitable figures are created for such occasions, if considered saleable. Coronations have always been occasions for bringing out appropriate figures, either entirely new or redesigned [figure 31].

For a long time the actual technique of hollow casting was held to be a family secret, and while it is now generally known, it still entails many years of experience to acquire the skill. Moulds are made from wax models, and a mixture of lead is heated in pots and poured into the moulds; after a few seconds, depending on the size and shape of the mould, the surplus lead is drained out, and when the mould is opened it turns out a casting [figure 33].

Mould 'flash' is removed, moveable arms are attached and the casting is given a dip in a special substance to improve paint adhesion. Painting in almost every case must be done by hand, only certain items such as vehicles and elephants being suitable for application by spray. The paint is tough and glossy, delighting children, but it is the despair

25

32 Part of a Punic elephant group made by the German modeller Heyde, c. 1906. In spite of the odd proportions, the group has a realistic effect: now in the Museum of Childhood, Edinburgh

33 (below) Messrs Britain's supplied the Author with these unpainted standard-size pieces, some of their 'Knights of Agincourt', designed for them by R. Selwyn Smith

of adult collectors. Vehicles and such items are stove finished in a gas fired oven.

As a family concern (the present head is the grandson of the founder) Britain's tend to keep their employees for life. Casting is done mostly by men and painting by girls and women who have been found to be more deft. 'Outwork' is done by married women who paint or assemble in their homes, a fleet of lorries taking consignments out and back. Within the economic limits imposed by the toy trade, Britain's always strive to make their figures as accurate as possible. The early figures can be identified by experts as coming from such outstanding military artists as Simkin and Harry Payne, and also from well-known portraits and photographs of the late Victorian and Edwardian periods. Much research has gone into later figures. Britain's always consult suitable authorities; when planning a new model cow for the farm series they sought the advice of the English Jersey Cow Association on body-structure and markings. For information on equipment and uniforms they invariably find the regiments, the War Office or foreign military attachés only too willing to help. The College of Heralds has been consulted on matters of armorial bearings more than once [figures 8 and 33]. Although primarily toy makers, Britain's are well disposed towards collectors. They ventured into production of figures painted for collectors before 1939, but found it unsuccessful, and now confine themselves to supplying collectors with unpainted castings and spare arms, weapons, instruments, etc.

No other toy soldier firm has rivalled Britain's in England. Many have come and gone, leaving a few interesting figures

to be seized on by collectors. One of the few firms to survive is J. Hill & Co., which was formed in 1900 by a former employee of Britain's. Because of this, many 'Johillco' varieties bear a marked resemblance to those of Britain's, although they also produced original and interesting figures such as a mounted field-marshal complete with baton, and a recent steel-helmeted figure with a small ring in lieu of a hand on the left arm for use with interchangeable weapons [figure 125]. For a brief period after the 1939-45 War, a firm, Malleable Mouldings of Deal, fitfully brought out a quality range of figures based on designs by the Swedish maestro Holger Eriksson. The production methods were novel, the plant and some moulds being brought from the United States to a remote part of Ireland where casting and painting was done by indigenous labour under a Swedish supervisor. The products were then shipped to England for marketing. Distribution was not effective, and after a period of adversity the management gave up the struggle, which was a tragedy for collectors, for although they were marketed as toys, the castings were of high quality [figures 101 and 102].

The United States was long dependent on importation of toy soldiers from the Old World. Early attempts by transient firms seem to have consisted of copies of Heyde's and Britain's, but a firm called Barclay made a few solid figures of World War I American troops as did the Warren Company, whose artillery and horses deserve mention. This latter firm were taken over about 1940 by Comet, which had previously marketed a few figures under the name of 'Brigadier'. After a period of war work on recognition models on various scales, this firm began to produce in 1946 a fine range in 55

34 A light Cavalryman of the Polish Imperial Guard, 1810, an immensely distinguished regiment; a model by General Angenot

mm size known as 'Authenticast', designed by Eriksson. However, with the transfer of its plant and moulds to Ireland, the output of soldiers by Comet ceased.

Apart from the classical examples referred to earlier, and the traditional peasant carving of most countries, the wooden soldier in various sizes has been a steady favourite and has

28

often been depicted in ballet and children's plays. Charlotte Brontë speaks of her family playing with wooden soldiers at Haworth Parsonage in 1829, where they provided a little gaiety in the lives of that austere family. Specially commissioned wooden soldiers were popular with the great, several German princes having large collections, but they were gradually ousted by the round lead soldiers. However, as a medium for important statuettes, wood is still favoured, and the plastic wood of today, sold in tubes, is popular with many private makers.

35 (*right*) An officer of the Mameluke squadron in the service of Napóleon, 1802. The squadron was part of the Guard. This model in painted wood is by General Angenot

Major Collections

TODAY, THE MODEL SOLDIER is a recognised art form in which to portray uniforms, equipment and military activity. The shape and style of the figures may vary from the delicate flat to the fully rounded, and the scale from 1/75th for diorama work to 1/32nd, or standard size. Historical Institutes and Museums now not only include examples of early models as objects of instrinsic interest, but set out deliberately to portray historical events by single figures, groups, or elaborate dioramas. Apart from their use in war games, model soldiers play a valuable part in many military establishments. At the Guards Depot in Pirbright, two large layouts are maintained for instruction in such important ceremonies as Guards of Honour and the Sovereign's Birthday Parade [figure 42]. These are direct descendants of the drill block sets, examples of which are to be seen in the National Army Museum, Sandhurst, and the Castle Museum, York.

The National Army Museum houses many treasures that fall within the scope of this book. One is 'Captain Rivière's military figures on a mechanical base for the practice of Company Drill'. Comprising four groups of wood figures, two inches high, mounted on tin bases, they can be set in line or 'form fours' (a now obsolete drill movement). The little drill squad with their red coats, black trousers, belts and shakos probably represented Rifle Volunteers. At the time it was produced (1860), there was a great rush of patriots to the Volunteer movement in England and such an ingenious functional aid must have been in great demand [figure 37].

A set of plaster equestrian figures, some twelve inches high, of the King's Dragoon Guards (now the Queen's Dragoon Guards) loaned to the National Army Museum by the regiment, includes a model of an officer of 1685, the year in which this regiment of horse was raised. The dress was reminiscent of the Restoration, with a marked Cavalier flavour, although the effeminacy, of which Antony a' Wood

36 An officer of the King's Dragoon Guards in the uniform of 1685. Painted plaster, twelve inches high

31

complained in 1663, had disappeared in the greater uniformity that the standing army had now acquired. This figure displays the feathered hat, the full bottomed wig, the scarlet coat with yellow facings, gold and silver trimmed, the bright steel cuirass, the gauntlet gloves, the waist sash and decorated *shabraque* or saddlecloth which are very much of the period. The stylish sash served a double purpose; apart from ornamentation it was intended as a sling to assist in carrying the wearer from the field should he be wounded [figure 36].

In the same group is a less flamboyant but still picturesque officer of 1799. The scarlet coat has been reduced to the waistline in front and the tail reaches only to the saddle. The cuirass has disappeared, although continental armies retained it until much later; the French Cuirassiers advancing against the German Army in 1914 wore breast and back plates. But the heavy jacked boots, useful in knee to knee shock tactics, are retained. Noteworthy is the headdress, a large bicorne soft hat. The British Army has never been able to make up its mind about its headgear. The cocked hat (of which this is one variation) survived the longest, from the early eighteenth century to the present day, when versions of it are worn in full dress by the Queen, the Medical and Veterinary officers, quartermasters of the Household Brigade, the Military Knights of Windsor and certain Officers of Royal Bodyguards. Even so, uncertainty remained, some cocking it up into two, and others three, corners; and it was never decided whether the bicorned variety should be worn square with the shoulders or fore and aft. Although its uselessness for the *arme blanche* had long been obvious, (the expression 'going for it bald-headed' de-

37 An example of the functional use of model soldiers is Captain Rivière's device for demonstrating drill movements, *c.* 1860. The wooden figures move on sliding bases

38 A group of three colour-bearers by Russell Gammage. (*left to right*) Prussian Guards in 1900, the Suffolk Regiment in 1815 and the Royal Fusiliers in 1914. The latter colour-bearer would normally be an officer

rives from the fact that the Marquis of Granby's hat and wig fell off at the beginning of the charge at Warburg in 1760), heavy cavalry clung to it up to the Peninsular War. This statuette also illustrates the cruel practice of docking horses' tails which persisted in England for a long time. The Army were at first opposed to it, and an Order prohibiting it was issued in 1764, but it continued as a civilian fashion, and when large numbers of horses were required in the Napoleonic Wars the order was rescinded [figure 40].

A striking and unique model in the museum is of George,

39 (below) A pikeman of the Royal Scots (The Royal Regiment) c. 1633. This wooden carving, twenty-four inches high, is by C. Pilkington Jackson, and is one of a set depicting period uniforms on display in Edinburgh Castle at the Royal Scots Museum

40, 41 (below, centre and right) Two interesting models in the National Army Museum, Sandhurst, England, illustrating period uniforms. (centre) An officer of the King's Dragoon Guards, 1799. (right) George, Graf Brown, Marquis of Sligo, of the Austrian Imperial Army, 1788. The model, by Helmuth Krauhs, is of plaster, with the uniform made of cloth and gold lace

Graf Brown, Marquis of Sligo, who was a *Feldzangmeister* in the Austrian Imperial Army. Fourteen inches high, made of stuff and plaster by Helmuth Krauhs, he is modelled in the dress of 1788, a blue-grey coat, waistcoat and cuffs and leg-wear of black and holding a half-pike. The figure has a remarkably fine facial expression, and it was presented to the National Army Museum in September 1960 by the Austrian Minister of Defence. [figure 41].

Silver was often used in the past for modelling soldiers for the rich but the tendency in later times was to confine the use of precious metals to special commemorative

42 Commercial soldiers are still used today at the Guards Depot for instructing young British Guardsmen in their ceremonial duties, such as Trooping the Colour

pieces like the silver Nile boat at Sandhurst. In the 1885 Campaign, Lord Wolseley offered a prize of one hundred pounds to the boat of troops that completed the passage of the Nile from Sarras to Debbeh in the shortest time. The victor was a boat of the 1st. Battalion the Royal Irish Regiment, the old 18th Foot (disbanded in 1922). To commemorate this achievement, the money was used on this graceful model which was made in London in 1885. It has been often said that Indian princes in the last hundred years had collections of model soldiers in gold and silver, but I have been unable to trace any. The most eminent British firms in the business have no records of supplying such model soldiers to their clients, among whom were the wealthiest of the rajahs and nabobs.

43 Silver model of a Nile boat in 1885

44 A field officer of the Royal Waggon Train, British Army 1811-13, made of barbola on a wire frame by J. F. Morrison

The Royal United Services Institution in London houses the most important public assembly of flats in Britain. Arranged in fifteen dioramas of British history from the Roman landings in 55 BC to the Normandy beaches in 1944, they are the work of many hands. Conceived by the great designer of flats, Otto Gottstein, with components assembled both in England and abroad, the original plan was upset by the racial policy of the pre-1945 German Government. In the event, many modellers, well known and unknown, combined to complete this model layout on the grand scale. His last work was to produce part of a series of dioramas illustrating Jewish history.

Pilkington Jackson is probably best known for his series of carvings of the Scottish Regiments displayed at Edinburgh Castle and elsewhere in Scotland. Illustrated here is his Pikeman of the Royal Scots, 1633 [figure 39]. Although the British Regular or Standing Army only dates from 1660, several regiments were formed before this. In 1633, Charles I authorised a request that a regiment of foot be raised in Scotland for service abroad. Regiments of foot, for all round protection, then consisted of equal numbers of musketeers and pikemen. On the Restoration, Charles II sent for this regiment and placed it at the head of the infantry of the line. Their distinguished ancestry has given rise to a legend that the Royal Scots can claim descent from a Roman Legion, and thus they gained the nickname 'Pontius Pilate's Bodyguard', but this is without foundation in fact.

In the Regimental Museum of the Staffordshire Regiment at Lichfield is a group of twelve figures, twelve inches high, depicting the uniform of the North Staffordshire Regiment from 1768 to 1918. Those illustrated [figures 46, 47] depict the full dress of a typical line regiment between 1868 and 1881. This was the period when army reforms had become a great national preoccupation following the Crimean War, and within twelve years there were seventeen Royal Commissions, eighteen Select Committees of the House of Commons, nineteen War Office Committees and thirty-five other committees on the policy and administration of the War Department.

Not the least of these reforms was the abolition in 1871 of the purchase of officer commissions in the cavalry and infantry. Previously wealth could buy promotion and the evasion of service in dull and unhealthy colonies. Beau Brummel, who served in the 10th Light Dragoons whilst they were at fashionable Brighton, promptly 'sold out'

45 A silver statuette of a drummer of the 1st Punjab Regiment, Pakistan Army, in the full dress of 1957. The model is ten inches high

when the regiment was ordered to Manchester on the grounds that 'he could not go on foreign service', and in the 1860's one infantry officer had 'exchanged' so often that when asked the name of his regiment said, 'I'm afraid I can't tell you that, Ma'am; all I know is that they have green facings and are stationed at Aldershot'.

As well as initiating Army reforms, the Crimean War stimulated a type of interesting Victoriana. Staffordshire pottery, a field for collecting in itself, which had begun to include portrait figures as far back as 1802, is rich in military figures from the Crimea onwards. Prices were generally low and thousands of figures were turned out. No less than six British generals, the British Commander-in-Chief and the French Marshal Arnaud were modelled. Napoleon III appears in a number of martial poses, one bold design showing him uncomfortably seated on a large pile of cannons and cannon balls. Several versions of Florence Nightingale exist, though none shows her with her celebrated lamp. The war correspondents' stories of hardship deeply stirred public sentiment, and a very popular piece was 'The Wounded Soldier' being helped by his sailor friend [figure 50]. Although the Staffordshire potteries continued to depict military heroes from Highland Jessie of the Indian Mutiny to Roberts and Kitchener of the Boer War, the Crimean period was their zenith. New techniques of finishing and painting had coincided with the war, but later products tended to be crude and unsatisfactory. Until recently, Staffordshire portrait figures have been neglected, but now their value as period pieces of characteristic pose and colour is beginning to be appreciated by more than one school of collectors.

In the Imperial War Museum in south-east London, there are many exhibits which arouse the collector's interest, particularly those dealing with the First World War. The Royal Horse Artillery team by H. H. Cawood creates a striking impression of the sturdy fortitude of both men and horses in the grim struggles of the Western Front. The railway mounting depicts the sheer weight of material to which both sides resorted in their efforts to end the deadlock of trench warfare. The mounting was originally made for Armstrong Whitworths, the armament firm; it was purchased by the Museum in 1921, and the figures were added by Cawood [figure 48].

The preservation of toys is now undertaken as part of social history, and the Museum of Childhood in Edinburgh is

dedicated to bygone articles of cultural or general interest to children on the lines of a folk museum. The section of toy soldiers includes wood, metals, plastics and fabrics. There are examples of old Continental styles such as Heyde leads, modern German and French plastics and 'ancient' and modern Britain's [figures 32, 51, 54].

In the Republic of Ireland at the Curragh Camp Military Museum, a collection of models depicting Irishmen in military history is in process of being formed. At present, the exhibits include models of the Pope and Papal Guards, the present Irish Army, disbanded Irish Regiments of the British Army, and the Irish Brigade in the service of France. Denied, after the Treaty of Limerick in 1691, the opportunity of serving in the British Army, Irish soldiers, under the great Sarsfield, moved to France where they continued

46, 47 Two examples of flat wooden painted cut-outs, each twelve inches high. The North Staffordshire Regiment 1868 and 1881

48 A diorama of a twelve-inch howitzer on railway mounting during the First World War in France. The figures on the extreme left include those of King George V and the Prince of Wales, added to the model by H. H. Cawood. It is now in the Imperial War Museum, London

49 A model of a thirteen-pounder Royal Horse Artillery gun and team, 1918. The model, by H. H. Cawood, is in the Imperial War Museum, London

50 The Crimean War of 1854-6, aroused popular interest in the Army. The Staffordshire potteries turned out thousands of models, among them this favourite piece, '*The Wounded Soldier*', with his sailor friend

to serve the Stuart cause for a hundred years. It is said that in that time nearly half a million Irishmen crossed the seas and 200,000 died fighting for causes not their own. According to an Irish legend, their souls returned in the form of the wild geese that flew in from the continent every year. Recognised as splendid fighters in the field, they were at times somewhat uncomfortable allies to be quartered in the peaceful countryside, and periodic complaints were made of their misbehaviour. There is a story that when one particular series of incidents was brought to the notice of the Roi Soleil himself, he sent for the Irish Brigade Commander, Count Dillon. His Majesty read out the list and at the end said, 'Your damned soldiers are more trouble to me than the rest of my army put together'. Dillon bowed in acknowledgement. 'Sire', he said, 'the enemy make the same complaint.' France has other than martial reasons to remember the Irish Brigade, for one veteran officer, Captain Hennessy, on his retirement founded a brandy business which is now world famous [figure 21].

FRANCE - The birthplace of the solid figure has a variety of styles to show the visitor today. A climb up the several hundred circular steps in the Arc de Triomphe rewards him with two displays in solid standard size; one of the Great War including a band of Chasseurs-à-pied, and the other a procession of the armies of the Republic and Empire. In the Musée de la Marine at the Palais de Chaillot there are a number of dioramas of the French Navy, including an unusual one of harbour life and another of the marines in the defence of Paris in 1870. The single figures include a naval officer on a horse, always a subject for comment.

It was here in 1960 that the French model soldier society

presented its thirteenth exhibition. Continuing for three months, it brought together the work of many makers and collectors, and provided a unique opportunity for visitors to see and admire the excellence of French models. Approximately three hundred exhibits were on display, ranging from single figures to dioramas. The arrangement and grouping showed great imagination, and some of the dioramas had a quality comparable with that of master painters figures 57 and 63].

In the Salon Ney at the Invalides is the model soldiers section of the Musée de l'Armée. This collection of many thousands of figures includes cardboard, flats and solids of varying sizes, some by Schmid of Strasbourg and including Würtz Jee's *Grande Armée*. The flats are the Ridder Collection of battle scenes and depict Austerlitz, Jena and Eylau. The English visitor will recognise a large selection of Britain's models, including some French Dragoons and the uncommon British Camel Corps of the 1880's with riders wearing dragoon helmets, red tunics and blue breeches.

At Compiègne there is a remarkable collection of models which was founded in 1927 by a local man, M. Alfred Ternisien, who presented his own collection of some 30,000 various kinds. It has since been augmented by other leading French collectors such as Laurent and Gritton. Dioramas claim attention here, particularly a French reply to the British Siborne Waterloo model by Laurent, who took eighteen years to construct it. It is thirty yards square, embodies twelve thousand Heinrichsen figures and depicts the last charge of the French on the British Squares. Another notable diorama depicts a parade of the French Army near Rheims before

51 A German composition figure, *c.* 1935. It is made of elastolin, an unstable composition that deteriorates with damp

52 An officer and Hussar of the French 2nd Regiment, 1804, previously known as the Esterhazy Hussars. It fought at Austerlitz, Friedland and Solferino. A carving in wood by General Angenot

53 One of Napoleon's aides-de-camps in field uniform, *c.* 1805. A brilliant carving in wood by General Angenot

54 (*right*) Some museums preserve toys as records of social history. This German 'scissors-toy' of 1910 survives in the Museum of Childhood, Edinburgh (Councillor Murray's Collection)

the Czar in 1901. The maker of this, Alfred Silhol, who actually took part in the review, used 12,000 semi-solids and spent thirty-two years on its construction.

Strasbourg deserves special mention because it is the centre for collectors of cardboard figures, which flourished in Strasbourg owing to its printing industry and the presence of a lively garrison. The first sets of printed card sheets of soldiers were issued by a certain Seyfried in 1744 to celebrate a visit by Louis XV. These were followed by others, the variety of troops and uniforms of the Revolution being faithfully reproduced. Improved processes such as lithography in the early twentieth century enabled output to be further increased with new publishers entering the market, and covering many periods and subjects. Although the product itself may be transient, the makers have shown great resilience. Output continued during German occupation of the area from 1870 with new collections, and during the Second World War somehow an 'underground industry' produced an army of eighty thousand! Strasbourg Museum contains many examples of cardboard figures.

In the Inter-Allied Museum at Arromanches there is an impressive diorama of the D Day landings in 1944. It was commissioned by Sir Winston Churchill from Messrs Stokes,

55 One of the new postwar German firms is Staar, which produces finely engraved 30 mm figures. These are examples of Louis XIV's troops from the firm's catalogue

56 In Ireland the collection at the Curragh Camp Military Museum includes this carriage of the President of Ireland. The carriage is wood-carved: the figures are conversions by the Author

57 Realistic dioramas of small groups are very popular in France and America. This group by the eminent modeller, Mme Metayer, is of Muzafer Singh at Pondicherry, India, in 1749

Greenwood and Ball, very well known artists in this medium, and was presented to the Museum by the British Government.

GERMANY - The heavy bombing inflicted on Germany in the Second World War and the actions of some occupation troops, coupled with the moral obloquy attached to the making of model war figures, have drastically reduced the previous wide interest in collections in Germany. The exception are flat figures which can be found in the collections which have either escaped destruction or which

58 It is possible to produce very lively groups from plywood. Horse artillery of the French Imperial Guard by R. North

59 Perhaps the greatest modern creator of flat figures is Otto Gottstein, who produced these lively mediaeval types

60 Highlanders in the snow, *c.* 1815 models by Russell Gammage. The 'snow' is a mixture of chalk, salt and alum

have been reconstructed. Post-war manufacture has tended to concentrate on the non-military and non-political such as ancient and social history and Red Indians and cowboys, but recent new varieties include Boers, Russians, Afrika Corps, and figures of the Queen's Birthday Parade.

As already noted, German interest, amounting to a passion, has always been centered on the flat, although there was a limited appreciation in some places of the solid. The flat is the genre which in the main has survived. Nowhere is there a finer collection than at the Deutches Zinnfig-

61 Collectors often commission special work from manufacturers. This Napoleonic Grenadier is by Peter Blum of New York

62 Officers of the German General Staff during the advance on Liège in 1914. The car is a Mercedes. Conversion by R. Dilley

urenmuseum, Plassenburg Castle, Külmbach, in Bavaria. Begun in 1931, the collection had reached a hundred thousand models by 1945, but depredations caused the museum to be closed, until it was again opened to the public in 1952. When an international conference was held there in 1957, the collection had risen to over twenty thousand and the remarkable number of 133 dioramas. The latter include scenes of early civic history, the life of the North American Indians and a layout of the old 1913 German Army Corps together with their Corps and Divisional flags and standards.

A rare museum collection of solids is that of Haffner figures in the Bayerisches National Museum, Munich. These

63 A superb group of models by Madame Metayer of the *Regiment Royal des Vaisseaux* at exercise, 1760 The background is painted by Lelipvre. Collection A. Gritton

consist of German military types of the 1830s. This museum also contains examples of the ancient military figures discussed in Chapter One. At Potsdam a number of dioramas are preserved, composed chiefly of civilian flats by the local maker, Meyerheine. There are also a few military scenes, but many of the moulds for these have been destroyed. In 1959 a collection of over twenty thousand pieces which had disappeared during the occupation was discovered in a cellar and returned to the Hersbruck Museum, near Nuremberg.

Of the dozen or so leading makers of 30 mm flat figures who exhibited at the famous Leipzig Exhibition in 1930,

64 A charging dragoon of the French Army about 1810, illustrating the dramatic effect obtainable by carving and painting wooden models. It is the work of General Angenot, the celebrated French modeller

only two have survived; the remainder, together with many lesser known, disappeared as a result of the 1939-45 war. These are Kiel (or Ochel) and Frauendorf of Halle. A few new firms have recently arisen of which the most noteworthy are Beck, Kebbel and Staar. All these firms (except Ochel) are very careful to concentrate on general subjects, mythology and classical history, and the artistry of design and execution entitle them to be highly prized [figure 55].

Since the end of the Second World War there have been a few exhibitions of dioramas held in West Germany, including one at Hanover in 1955 and another at Weimar in 1956. Various authorities collaborated by lending exhibits. The Weimar exhibition inclined towards scenes of civil life such as incidents from *Die Meistersinger* and an eighteenth century chamber concert, although a few single

65 A group of Union troops in the American Civil War. (*left*) An officer and drummer of the 'Iron Brigade' and (*right*) two privates of the New York Zouaves, by Norman Newton Ltd

historic figures were shown. At Hanover, the exhibition contained some twenty-five thousand figures as well as pictures and uniforms.

German societies ceased to exist as a result of the last war, but a number of new ones have come into existence in West Germany in the last few years. They embrace all types of figures as well as soldiers. One society now has six hundred members but it is estimated that there are thousands of collectors who do not belong to societies. In East Germany there is a society, and figures are made by different 'editors'. Scholtz still produces all the old types, as well as many new, examples of which occasionally get through the Iron Curtain.

THE UNITED STATES - The newly–found interest in collections of model soldiers is spreading so quickly throughout

America that it is difficult to catalogue the principal exhibits and centres of interest. The national predilection for fraternity activity has stimulated the formation of many societies, some of which are now internationally known and others of more local character. American pursuit of the hobby is characterised by a zeal for accuracy, a desire for friendly co-operation and exchange of ideas, and an urge to make up for lost time. At the time of writing, collecting seems to be most developed in the Eastern and Western States with the mid-continental States just becoming aware of it.

The Museum of the City of New York has a collection of seventeen miniature figures, each about nine inches high. These are extremely lively and realistic figures depicting military units raised in New York from the early Burgher Guard of 1640 to an Infantry Sergeant of a New York unit in World War Two. New York is very proud of its local military tradition, and British visitors will be pleased to see the Royal

66 A group of officers and ratings of the Royal Navy, and one Royal Marine. The figures were converted by the Author from Britain's and Malleable Mouldings models

67 The Emperor Napoleon, by General Angenot. This beautiful model of the Emperor in campaigning dress before he grew stout is made up of many materials. The horse is of wood

68 German flat figures of 1930s. Troops of Frederick the Great by Ochel, which, with Franendorf of Halle, was one of the two German firms to survive the Second World War

American Regiment of 1755, now the 60th Rifles. It is remarkable to observe how the European styles of each period were followed, such as the shako and coatee of the early nineteenth century, the Zouave vogue, the universal hussar style and a uniform inspired by highland dress. Also in the New York Museum are some examples of crude wood (American and Bavarian), cardboard Rough Riders (American), German solids and early Britain's.

The US Military Academy at West Point has a valuable collection of figures. There are twenty-one plaster figures, of the history of Cadets' uniforms, designed for the Museum by the US Quartermaster General's Office in Washington. There is also a large group of Metayer models of Napoleon with his Old Guard, five dioramas by various artists depicting Crecy, Cynoscephalus and battles of the American continent. That of the Battle of Gettysburg made by the US Army Exhibits Unit is a particularly striking piece of work. The size of the figures, varying from four to eight inches, enabled the artists to create some splendid facial expressions which reveal to the student as much pictorial history as the photographs of Brady or Gardner. Here in these little figures can be seen the weariness and the bitter disappointment of the charge that almost succeeded. Preceded by the unusual event of an artillery barrage, the tide of Confederate Gray had crashed against Federal Blue but had been unable to swamp it. It was a turning point in the most tragic conflict ever engaged by American soldiers— the Civil War [figure 70]. West Point also has five cloth figures, each fourteen inches high, specially made by Helmuth Krauhs, of Confederate troops with Lee and representative officers, and enlisted men of cavalry, infantry and artillery [figure 69].

Amongst the exhibits at the United States Naval Academy at Annapolis is a sculpture in miniature by Dwight Franklin on permanent display in the museum. It is an artist's original conception, and Captain Ross F. Collins, USA (Rtd) has supplied the following description:

'This sculpture group represents the peak of Paul Jones's career as captain of the old *Bon Homme Richard* in his fight with HMS *Serapis* off Flamborough Head. With two of his six 18-pounders exploding at the first discharge and tearing out the deck and part of the side, and only a few light 9-pounders in action, the ship filling fast and two hundred prisoners manning the pumps being held there at pistol-point, Captain Pearson called to Jones, "Have you struck?"

Jones bellowed back: "No, I have not yet begun to fight". With the upper decks about to collapse into the hold, and on fire near the magazine, and seven feet of water in the hold, he continued to fight. Captain Pearson, with a shattered gun deck and nearly half his crew killed or wounded, hauled down his flag. Jones transferred his survivors to the *Serapis*, and next morning the *Bon Homme Richard* drove to the bottom.

'The group is 45 x 72 x 30 inches. Although 72 inches high, the glass in front is not more than 30 inches, but as you peer inside and look up you see the masts and sails towering upward. Jones is about 7-inches tall. There are fourteen figures. The men on the poop are French Marines. The gun by Jones is a 9-pounder and is about 10 inches overall. It is the one he was personally directing at the mainmast of *Serapis*. Ship and guns are wood and canvas with metal fittings. The figures are modelled in a mixture of plaster and wax, beautifully coloured in proper detail.'

The Smithsonian Institution in Washington at present holds in the Marine Corps section two historical groups which are unusual in that each is the work of a husband and wife, Mr and Mrs C. Wirth and Mr and Mrs G. Harle. American Society bulletins and literature record several instances of such partnerships.

The United States has taken well to the diorama, but this term has not the same rigid meaning as in Europe, and it is not confined to the flat figure as is often the case in the Old World. Many American dioramas contain only a few figures in contrast to the European fashion of including as many as possible. A further interesting development is to emphasise perspective by using 22, 16, and 8 inch figures reading from the front in that order. Between 1948 and

69 Another example of a modern model in cloth, leather and metal, one of a series in West Point Museum by Helmuth Krauhs of Vienna

70 A vivid diorama of the American Civil War. The retreat of Pickett's Division on the third day of the Battle of Gettysburg, 1863; Pickett reports to Lee. Constructed by the US Army Exhibits Unit, West Point Museum, Virginia

71 American Marines spiking the guns of a French fort in Santo Domingo, 11 May 1800. Models made of bees-wax with wood and metal additions, at the Marine Corps Memorial Museum, Philadelphia

1956, one society staged five exhibitions in Philadelphia and in these several new display forms were tried out.

SOUTH AND CENTRAL AMERICA - Activity in Mexico, at present, seems to be left to one concern which produces standard size figures of Aztecs and other period figures. The quality is not high, probably because there is little cultural interest in the subject. In South America there is a considerable market, and Garratt has identified at least six firms in the Argentine alone. Their production seems to be mainly copied from European designs and scales, although one firm produced such local heroes as Bolivar, O'Higgins and San

72 The first use of aircraft to evacuate wounded under fire, at Quilali, Nicaragua, in 1928, when eighteen American Marines were flown out. The model was constructed by Sgt W. F. Gemeinhardt USMC

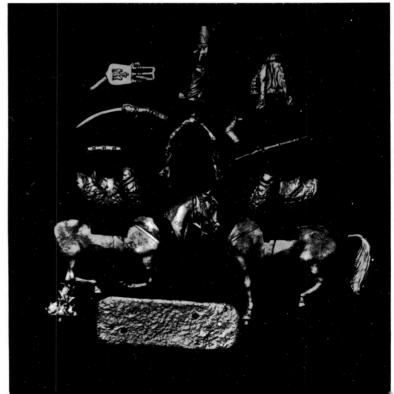

73 (*left*) 'Surrender? I have not begun to fight.' Paul Jones yells defiance from the *Bonne Homme Richard*. A diorama constructed by Dwight Franklin at the US Naval Academy, Annapolis

74 (*right*) Some 'custom-made' castings are sold unassembled to collectors. These American pieces form a Napoleonic Hussar 54 mm in height

75 An officer of the Fourth Light Dragoons in 1822, by Russell Gammage, an English modeller with a rising reputation

76 (left) A wounded Prussian Hussar, c. 1914, made by Norman Newton Ltd. These figures have few equals in their particular field

Martin. Semi-flats are also plentiful and are to be found in Peru, Bolivia and Chile; designs and paintings aim to cover all local civil wars which would seem to provide scope for a very large market.

BELGIUM - The Royal Museum of Military History in Brussels has recently acquired a small collection of lead soldiers. In Bruges, in the Musée Gruuthuse, there is an interesting collection of late eighteenth-century moulds representing Austrian cavalry and infantry. Before the Second World

77 Scene on Red Beach, Tarawa Atoll, 13th November 1943, showing the landing of the US Second Marine Division. The model is made of duron with some wood by Displayers Inc., New York

War, reproductions of these were made and an unpainted set of each type (twenty-eight) is in the Musée de l'Armée in Brussels.

Belgium appears to have only one indigenous producer of models, the Steinbeck firm, trade mark 'MIM', which produced solid figures of excellent quality. Beginning a few years before World War Two, production ceased in 1948, and Belgian collectors of model soldiers once more rely on imports. Both flats and solids are popular. Two societies flourish in Belgium, each publishing its own bulletin.

DENMARK - As noted elsewhere in this account, a Dane is honoured as the father of the literature of the model soldier, yet until recently there appears to have been little interest in Denmark. There is a small society, one member of which has a large collection of flats of the 1815 period, but no public collections are known. The Danish Folk Museum exhibits one flat 5-cm model knight believed to date from 1800, and a flat portrait model of King Frederick VII, mounted, 15 cm high, circa 1850, but the authorities are unable to identify the makers of either figure. Only one

78 The art of the diorama has reached one of its highest points in the United States. Here US Marines attack Mexico City, 1847. Model by Displayers Inc., New York

maker of the past is known, 'Hoy', from whom a single mould for flats is preserved, dated 1850. Currently there are several firms engaged in producing models, two in solids, one in flats, one in aluminium and one in plastic. The scales vary from the old Heyde for the solids to 75 mm for the aluminium. Reports as to quality vary except in the case of the flats which, as frequently in this kind of figure, have attracted a clever designer to execute them.

HOLLAND - Holland has never had a native production of models, either flats or solids, and relies entirely on importation. In 1955 a society was formed under the name of Stichting ter Bevordering van de Toepassing van Culturhistorische Tinne Figuren, or STBVDTVCTF for short. The members quickly began to make up for lost time and in 1956 organised an exhibition at the Weigh House, Amsterdam. Such was their initiative that the exhibition was supported by all the principal model soldier countries including Britain, France and USA. A number of privately made models by members were displayed which were of high quality and interest can now be expected to grow in the Netherlands.

79, 80 Collectors tend to specialise in their choice of figures. Glenn Thompson's collection is devoted to state body-guards of the world. Here are his conversions of a Guard Hussar and (*right*) an officer in the Danish Royal Life Guards

ITALY - Although the makers are unknown, flat figures were manufactured in Italy at least as early as the eighteenth century. In the Museo del Commune in Milan there is a large collection of flats dating from about 1770, consist-

SCANDINAVIA - Norway exhibits some unknown peasant carvings in the Norsk Folkemuseum, Oslo; and at Ledaal (Stavanger) there are a number of flats and solids which Garratt believes to be of German origin. There is a small but interested society which appears to rely mostly on imports, since the only products of native makers are mostly of the farm range and of indifferent quality. In Sweden, at the Uppsala University Institute, there is a collection representative of Gustavus Adolphus. Professor Rössner, a designer of flats, and therefore with an understandable bias in favour of this style, explains the absence of model soldiers from museums in Sweden by the fact that curators have not yet decided whether the collection of representative figures is worthwhile. There appears to be little demand toing of 1 inch infantry and 1½ inch mounted men. In the Museo Civico in Turin there are some hundred infantry, cavalry and artillery models of the old Sardinian army. Currently flat figures are being produced by one firm in

81 (*right*) An officer of the Fourth Light Dragoons, *c.* 1822, made by Russell Gammage

82 (*far right*) A Private of a British line Regiment fixing his bayonet, *c.* 1860. By Russell Gammage

83 (*below*) A Swedish soldier by a Swedish master modeller. The model is of a soldier of the Royal Lifeguards, and is painted by Glen Thompson, to whose collection it belongs

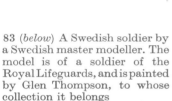

Rome. Solid figures do not appear ever to have been popular, and attempts to produce them have mostly failed, only two small firms being in production, one with Napoleonic and the other with a more catholic range. Italians have been more interested in paper and card figures on sheets. These have been made from the 1870's onwards, and are still an attraction for Italian collectors. In the Naples Museum there is a collection of cardboard figures, heightened with gold and mounted on wooden blocks. They are of high quality and it is thought that they were made for the King of Naples as they exceed other known examples both in design and finish. There is no society for model soldier collectors, but many are members of the Unione Nazionale Collezionisti d'Italia.

day for military figures as toys, and as a result no commercial firm is producing soldiers. In the past there were three firms (Santessonka Tenngjuteriet, Schreuder and Olsson Leksaksfabrik, and Tenngjuteriet Mars) who between them pro-

84 A Spanish model by Captain Carlos Martinez-Valverde of an Arquebusier of the Army of the Sea of Naples, c. 1566. The material is solid metal and the height 45 mm

duced a range of flats and solids in varying scales and qualities from 1843 to the 1930's. However, due to the presence of that master designer, Holger Eriksson, there is a lively if limited group of private specialist makers. The Eriksson school specialises in solids, both in the 54 mm scale and latterly in 40 mm. Professor Georg Rössner has influenced local collectors and induced one to go into business with him in the production of flats. A life-long collector and a practical engraver for about thirty years, Professor Rössner came from Germany in 1945; like many collectors who create their own figures either by conversion or casting, his aim is to combine historical accuracy with the personal touch.

SPAIN - 'Lead soldiers provided the main entertainment of many children, rich and poor, during the nineteenth century and reproductions of animals sometimes cast in lead, sometimes carved in wood, were of wonderful realism.' So wrote the author of *El Arta Popular en Espana*.

In Barcelona there are displays in two museums. In the Museo de Industrias y Artes Populares del Pueblo Español there is an unusual display of early nineteenth-century moulds, including, as well as soldiers, religious figures, dancers, animals, ships and vehicles. In the Museo de Historia de la Ciudad there is a religious procession of over one hundred flat figures. In Madrid, there are also two museums with displays; the Museo del Ejercito has 400 carved wood figures by Senor Tello, and the Naval Museum possesses marine figures by a skilled private craftsman of today, Captain Carlos Martinez-Valverde. Further models by him are at the Military-Naval School and two other military establishments [figures 84 and 87].

Spanish commercial production has been chequered. The nineteenth-century vogue for soldiers appears to have languished, since all the moulds and models of one interesting firm were destroyed in the Civil War of 1936. At present, one firm markets 40 mm lead soldiers in very attractive imitation bookcase wrappers, several produce plastic figures and there is also a small output of cardboard sheets. A society was formed in Barcelona in 1960.

SWITZERLAND - The Zürich Landesmuseum houses a comprehensive collection of Swiss flats, and there is a Swiss society, the 'Friends of the Tin Soldier', in Zürich with a current membership of about forty. Since the war production appears to have been in the hands of a private

85 Modern Italian figures of metal, 40 mm high, excellently painted, representing the famous Bersaglieri

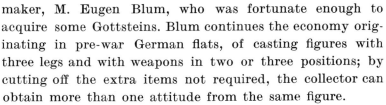

86 Italian ambulance figures of the early twentieth century. The horses and drivers are flats, and the vehicles of painted wood

maker, M. Eugen Blum, who was fortunate enough to acquire some Gottsteins. Blum continues the economy originating in pre-war German flats, of casting figures with three legs and with weapons in two or three positions; by cutting off the extra items not required, the collector can obtain more than one attitude from the same figure.

ELSEWHERE - Japanese figures are not very important, being mostly blatant piracies of European and American models. When Garratt enquired into the position in occupied Poland, it seemed that authority was inclined to be contemptuous of the hobby, and the few figures exhibited since then have neither taste nor artistry. Russia, of course, has a long peasant tradition for wooden figures, and cardboards were also popular. The Hermitage in Leningrad displays some eighteenth-century flat wood cut-outs, part of Peter III's collection. Pre-revolution commercial lead output was of flats, poorly made, very brittle and gaudily painted. Some miniature soldiers are made in Russia at the present time by toy-making co-operatives and factories. Steel helmeted Russian troops with their equipment appeared at the Leipzig Toy Fair in 1957.

87 Another model by Captain Martinez-Valverde, showing a Spanish naval commandant, c. 1808. At this period there was a shortage of ships, and naval officers took part in the fighting on land

63

Collecting Today

THE PREVIOUS CHAPTER GAVE a glimpse of what might be called the public side of the model soldier of today. This chapter attempts to tell of the activity of the private collector, what sources are open to him and how he can create his own models.

Collections can be built up in three ways: by the purchase of what Garratt aptly describes as the connoisseur figure; by relying on the output of the toy makers; or by making or converting for oneself. There is no doubt that the latter is the most satisfying. In practice the collector resorts to all three methods, and the size and quality of his collection will be decided by financial considerations, the availability of suitable toys, and his own standards of taste, knowledge and craftsmanship. There is no clear dividing line between maker and collector, buyer or seller; some of the leading makers have entered the industry partly to satisfy their own requirements, and many amateurs make figures or parts for fellow amateurs in exchange for other figures made by them.

My own method of collecting may serve as a typical example of this involved situation. When I grew up, my battered toy soldiers were left in boxes, without any thought to their future. On an occasional visit to a museum or exhibition I was surprised to see that model soldiers were prized exhibits, particularly some which were obviously similar to my veterans but rebuilt and repainted to a high standard. A tour of duty in London made me familiar with the displays in the Royal United Service Institution, and with the high-grade model soldier then beginning to appear in London shops. Any further thoughts of making a collection of my own were then interrupted by a real war (with none of the pomp and glamour of the tin soldier) and my energies were absorbed by my part in it.

After the war, when I turned to the study of military history as a serious interest, it occurred to me that model soldiers could be a good medium for illustration. I began

88 The Colour Party of the Gloucestershire Regiment in 1914, from the collection of Colonel C. W. A. Bath

65

to consider my rabble of toy soldiers as the nucleus of a collection. I joined a society, frequently visited London (the British Mecca of the model soldier world) and was lured into shops to buy figures I could not afford. After two to three years I had a number of good figures, but they had no central theme, they represented nothing, and they did not amount to a collection. To obtain the all-important balance, I consulted various specialists and private makers; this enabled me to commission a number of the varieties I wanted. I was now able to specify the regiment, period, dress, rank and to some extent the attitude and position. I soon realised, however, that if I wanted to have a collection based on my own ideas, I would have to do most of the creative work myself. I was considering at this time, in conjunction with a kindred spirit, what military men call an 'order of battle', a complete list of the regiments, headquar-

89 (*below*) Artillery and infantry with drums and fifes at St James Palace, London, *c.* 1800, by W. Corman. The tin figures are cast from slate moulds, a technique suitable for flats or semi-flats

90 The Royal Artillery in 1815, the year of Waterloo, bringing a nine-pounder gun into action. The figures are cast with separate heads, arms and equipment, which plug into the body and are made of a mixture of kaolin and lead. Exhibited by Russell Gammage in 1961

ter staffs, corps and services, the types of officers and men, how they would be depicted, the vehicles and accessories necessary to portray my model army, and it amounted to some 5,500 pieces. A rough estimate of cost made it apparent that I could only realise my ambition by becoming a converter on a big scale. So, my plan is now based on mixing the three sources: an occasional connoisseur figure from a shop, (providing it fits into the establishment), contracting and exchanging with fellow collector-makers, and producing my own figures by conversion from suitable toys.

The model soldier connoisseur is like a collector of pictures. He is a knowledgeable man who is either too busy or lacks the skill to create his own models, but desires the best. He is provided for by the top modellers of Paris and London. These are the masters who make what they enjoy most, cater only for a very exclusive market, and charge accordingly. Probably the leader in this class in Roger Berdou of France. He specializes in mounted figures, eight cm high, of the First Empire. They exude an *élan*, a definite air of France,

91 The Author's models displayed at Edinburgh for the 1961 Festival Tattoo. A mechanism was incorporated which caused the massed bands to march and countermarch. The figures in left foreground are of Royal Norwegian Guards which appeared in that year's tattoo

92 A Yeomanry headquarters *c.* 1910, including the General Officer Commanding and officers of different British regiments

which gives them an added attraction for the foreigner.

Many collectors consider Richard Courtenay's standard size mediaeval figures the finest of their kind, for their lively action as well as the brilliance of the heraldic colourings on which Courtenay is regarded as a world authority. Garratt, whose opinions deserve to be taken seriously by collectors, considers Ping, another British modeller, to be among the world masters. 'A Ping is a projection into the past, the figure (taken, as it may well be, directly from the original monument, brass or illustration) lives again in the century in which it was conceived. He visualizes his figures in terms of quietude, with the result that despite their trappings, they still retain dignity and calm.' Ping's sets of figures to illustrate the film *Richard III* are typical exam-

93 The eagle of the First Tirailleurs Algériens, captured and burnt at the Battle of Sedan in 1870. Broumes Collection, Paris

ples of his craft. Representative of a small number of British makers and a modeller whose work is rapidly acquiring international status, is Russell Gammage. His work is characterized by great accuracy and fine detail while at the same time his lively and inventive mind has produced new methods and materials, for example, the figures made in malleable lead which can be easily bent to alternate positions. In my opinion, one of his finest figures is a mounted officer of the Fourth Light Dragoons, 1822, inspired by an oil painting by J. Pardon. The figure, dressed in light and dark blue with yellow facings, generously laced with silver and surmounted by an imposing plume of white and scarlet cock's feathers on an extremely tall shako, gives an impression of richness and grandeur. For a designer to spend his

94 Two figures of women. (*left*) A member of the First Aid Nursing yeomanry in full dress *c.* 1908; and (*right*) a nursing sister in the Second World War, Conversions by R. S. Dilley

95 The converter creates his models with a background of long familiarity with military history and military types. This conversion was based on the Principal Director of music, Royal Marines, and is by the Author

time making such a very intricate model, consisting in eighteen separate parts, of an unfashionable period was almost foolhardy, particularly as every part had to be made new and could not be converted from any existing pieces. However the model *was* made, and captured the imagination of the collectors, and more were sold than of any other mounted figure. The horse was cast in four parts: two sides, a head and a tail. The base was of heavy tinned steel stamped with holes to take studs on the hooves. The rider's body, head, arms, and sword and *sabretache* were all cast as separate pieces fitted together with pegs. The *shabraque* was stamped out of sheet tin-lead alloy, and the reins and harness were cut from shim copper. The bits were cast from tin [fig. 75].

'Highlanders in the Snow' [figure 60], consists of all standard tin alloy figures, made in pieces but with the body cast in a marching position on a base. The bases would detract from the pictorial value of the group, so it was decided to show them on the march on a snow-covered landscape, which effectively covered the offending bases. The snow was a mixture of French chalk, salt and alum. The 42nd were first raised as the 43rd Highland Regiment of Foot, and were formed to help General Wade police the Highlands. They have fought gallantly all over the world as over forty honours in their colours bear testimony. The uniforms shown are of the time of Waterloo.

In America there are now so many competent specialist model makers that it is difficult to select any as better than the remainder; my personal preference is equally divided between the work of Brady, Bussler and Imrie, of whom I have more knowledge than the others. Garratt also commends the work of Vertunni, now dead, whose widow resides in Italy.

In Britain, after the last war, there was an acute shortage both of connoisseur figures of the kind wanted by the discriminating collector, and also of commercial models worthy of conversion. In this period the models of W.Y. Carman partly filled the gap. As an recognised military historian and the exhibits director of a war museum, he was able to bring first-hand knowledge to the design of his figures, and if they were not of the highest quality, they were most reasonable in price and many collectors owe him a debt of gratitude. This 'Carbago' range included flats by Otto Gottstein, but troubles arose as a result of purchase tax classification, (the period was a most difficult one for the production of anything which the authorities could define as a 'luxury'),

96 (*above*) The mounted band of the Fifth Royal Inniskilling Dragoon Guards in full dress, a Britain's conversion by R. Dilley and the Author, in the Author's collection

and the promising venture was terminated. Later R. Briton Rivière acquired some of them and added to the range. This modeller's work, now in hard plaster, is known to collectors as 'Matchlock'.

In France there is an important group of modellers whose excellent work is not beyond the average collector's pocket; typical of these is Madame Metayer. There were many examples of modern French work on display in the 1960 Exhibition at the Palais de Chaillot [figures 57 and 63].

It is at the exhibitions, of course, that the work of the private maker can be discovered and examined, not only

97 (*right*) Changing the guard at Aldershot Cavalry Barracks, *c.* 1900. The guardroom cat and the fire-buckets add a realistic touch to the scene. Conversions by R. S. Dilley and the Author, in the Author's collection

98 A Captain of the Royal Army Service Corps, *c.* 1918, made of barbola by J. F. Morrison

by collectors but by an interested public. Exhibitions not only stimulate the modeller who already makes for a clientele but gives an opportunity to the many truly private modellers who convert or mould for their own pleasure or for a few friends. In the field of large exhibitions, the enterprise of the newly formed Dutch society has already been mentioned. Two international conferences have been held at Kulmbach since it has been restored and at least three large public displays in Germany. An American Society held five exhibitions in one State capital in eight years, and Spain and France have both held national exhibitions recently. The only exhibition of this rank directly sponsored by the British society was the Waterloo Commemoration Exhibition held in mid-1961 and this, as its name implies, was restricted in its display of models.

Societies vary in character according to their membership. Where it is a society mainly of private modellers, the emphasis is on research and a library and reference service; where membership includes collectors who like to buy their figures, these societies often include a sales section to meet this requirement. Many collectors who live too far from the societies' meeting places, band themselves into informal groups, either of a local nature or because they share a particular interest. This form of communion has advantages, as the members are stimulated by other common interests and ideas flow rapidly between them. They pool resources and techniques, and some of the more exciting amateur work, especially in conversion, comes from them. This type of collection building is probably the most satisfying but calls for specialised knowledge of the subjects to be modelled as well as some skill in handicraft.

To be satisfying, the figures or groups must be an extension of what one knows or has seen, so they tend to be (as in all forms of original art) what the maker or interpreter sees in them. To me, a horse is a thing of great natural beauty with its elegant head, silken mane, a tail and a well-proportioned body. If it is an officer's horse, it will be of better breed than that required in the troop, but there is more to it than just these simple differences. The horse is a creature of great liveliness; although schooled and trained to steadiness to a high degree, it shows its spirit by the set of its ears, the occasional movement of a foot, or the switch of the tail. For me, a line of model horses all with their heads, legs and tails in rigid one-style positions, fails to reproduce the feeling of the originals. Whoever saw twelve or eighteen horses all remain in the same position for even a moment! The inquisitive look around, the bad-tempered try to nip someone, the vain or restless throw up their heads, the sophisticated rest a hoof. So, with models one must try to capture this sense of animation by a variation of the figures by changing the heads, or merely bending them out of the mould position, and by similar actions with the legs and tails.

One of the most brilliant amateur converters known to me obtains startling results by merely altering the position of one limb of a figure and possibly changing its head. But before these simple operations could be carried out, he made a long study of the regimental history and the cam-

99 Lord Chelmsford and his staff. The sand in the model was taken from the trenches of the battlefield of Tel-el-Kebir. The figures are conversions by R. S. Dilley from Britain's and Hill's originals

100 (*below*) Highland Regimental signallers of the 42nd Scottish Regiment (Black Watch) on exercise, *c.* 1900. Britain's conversions by R. S. Dilley in the Author's collection

101, 102 (*above*) Two mounted officers, *c.* 1900 by R. S. Dilley. (*left*), a mounted field officer of the Seaforth Highlanders, a Malleable Mouldings conversion. (*right*) the Commanding Officer of the 32nd Lancers, Indian Army, a Britain's conversion by R. S. Dilley and the Author

paign concerned, looked up photographs in contemporary magazines and journals, and gave it much intensive thought. On his way to and from work, my friend mentally builds, rejects and rebuilds in his mind's eye his conception of the basic figure. When this is decided, he concentrates on finding the attitude which will not only animate it but give it a sense of period. Completion is then comparatively easy as all his ideas about the figure are ready in his mind [figures 94, 95 and 96].

A collector in the west of England has described how he came to create his present collection:

'I have, over the years, collected and painted nearly six thousand pieces. These are of all kinds, but in the main British Army units. At the beginning, I decided to collect and make units so that I would have representatives of every unit (in full dress) in the British Army as it was in 1914. I collected and painted 'sets', that is, fourteen other-rank infantry with one foot and one mounted officer; cavalry, eight troopers, one Trumpeter and one officer; artillery, one gun team of each type. As the years went by I added Indian, Egyptian, Sudanese, Australian, New Zealand, British West Indies sets etc – both foot and mounted troops.

'Having got all these, I then realised that no formation

103 The Royal Engineers pioneered aviation in the British Army from the 1870s onwards. A balloon, and winch-wagon, *c.* 1890-1912, such as was used in the Boer War, now in the Author's collection

was suitable for display purposes, so cavalry was increased to one officer, one trumpeter and twelve troopers, and infantry to one mounted officer, two dismounted officers and twenty-eight rank-and-file. It was whilst in the process of this doubling-up that the toy makers on whom I am dependent decided to cease selling lead figures to the home market...'

WAR GAMES - Chess is the best known of all war games, and chessmen have been produced from many materials and in a great variety of styles, including the military. One of the more outstanding of these is an ivory set, to a three-inch size, depicting the combatants of the Battle of Agincourt. The American authority on model soldiers, Bob Bard, has a set of cast-iron chessmen in which the kings are Napoleon and Frederick the Great, and the bishops are represented by Old Guard or Prussian Grenadier Officers. By the time chess became a form of relaxation for Commanders the War Game was being developed as an aid to current military thought. Towards the end of the eighteenth century a German military theoretician, George Vinturinus, transferred the game from a chess board to a squared chart. Another German thinker, Von Reisswitz, developed a War Game further on a terrain model and published rules for it in 1824. The Emperor was so impressed by the Game that, due to his influence, it was introduced formally into the German Army.

Under the Duke of Cambridge, the British Army became interested and its first rules were published in 1872. Unfortunately, the Boers refused to fight according to these rules, and instead of revising them the British Army lost faith in the War Game. The Germans, however, maintained their interest, and the War Game continued to have such famous sponsors as von Moltke and von Schlieffen. It was used to test offensive strategy for the First World War, and played an important part as a training aid for the reviving German Army, and was later used to try out the initial offensives against France and the Soviet Union. In 1954, War Games were revived in the British Army as a research tool and entrusted to the Army Operational Research Group, a scientific body which advises the Army Council.

NURSERY-FLOOR WARFARE - The Game has also been followed less seriously by laymen. Robert Louis Stevenson has recorded a series of battles in which he and his stepson manoeuvred lead soldiers, and Laurence Sterne wrote of Uncle

Toby, an old soldier, who with his servant, Corporal Trim, followed Marlborough's Campaigns with a war game on a map.

Looking back on his early life, Winston Churchill has told how a primitive form of nursery-floor warfare began to shape his career:

'I was now embarked on a military career. This orientation was entirely due to my collection of soldiers. I had ultimately nearly fifteen hundred. They were all of one size, all British, and organised as an infantry division with a cavalry brigade. My brother Jack commanded the hostile army. But by a Treaty for the Limitation of Armaments he was only allowed to have coloured troops; and they were not allowed to have artillery. Very important. I could muster myself only eighteen field guns—beside fortress pieces. But all the other services were complete—except one. It is what every army is always short of — transport. My father's old friend, Sir Henry Drummond Wolff, admiring my array, noticed this deficiency and provided a fund from which it was to some extent supplied.

'The day came when my father himself paid a formal visit of inspection. All the troops were arranged in the correct formation of attack. He spent twenty minutes studying the scene—which was really impressive—with a keen eye and a captivating smile. At the end he asked me if I would like to go into the Army. I thought it would be splendid to command an army, so I said "Yes" at once; and immediately was taken at my word. For years I thought my father with his experience and flair had discerned in me the qualities

104 An Irish Colonel of Infantry and Commander of Air Corps discuss the principles of war 1930-50. Models by the Author in the Curragh Military Museum, Ireland

105 A British Army scene in the 1890s; an officer goes home. All these figures are converted from Britain's, Malleable Mouldings, Crescent and Charbens, showing the variations that an enthusiast can achieve

of military genius. But I was told later that he had only come to the conclusion that I was not clever enough to go to the Bar. However that may be, the toy soldiers turned the current of my life. Henceforward all my education was directed to passing into Sandhurst, and afterwards to the technical details of the profession of arms. Anything else I had to pick up for myself.'

The War Game as played by amateurs at this time was very destructive, with the little warriors being bombarded by catapults, pea-shooters and marbles. It is another man of genius, H. G. Wells, whom we find introducing rules which form the basis for those in use today. In 1908, the toy soldier makers, Britain's, had brought out a pamphlet *The Great War Game for boys of all ages, five to seventy-five years.* This contained rules for 'setting out the battlefield, the armies, mounting of troops, time, ammunition, casualties, prisons, tactics, and even war correspondents'. From his autobiography it seems that H. G. Wells held strong views on the cure for real wars; he advocated 'putting this prancing monarch and that silly scaremonger... into one vast Temple of War with cellars full of little trees, houses and soldiers, and leaving them there'. The Britain's pamphlet possibly inspired him to carry out various intellectual exercises, the first result of which was *Floor Games*. Published in 1911, it is mainly about civilian games but includes some references to model soldiers. In 1913, there appeared the famous *Little Wars* which codified Wells' ideas on 'a game that may be played by two or four or six amateurish persons in one afternoon and evening with toy soldiers'. A drawing of Wells, with his two brothers and Jerome K. Jerome, appeared in a London journal.

Wells' lethal ideas held the field until the realisation that there could be more to the game than destruction. Nowadays, most societies have model rules for war games in which the dice regulates tactics and administrative moves, and a carefully laid out battlefield is essential. Such precision has also called for uniformity in the size of the figures with a tendency towards diminution, the 1½ and 3 inch solids being the favourite. In America, the game has become

107 A Bavarian artillery officer in full dress, *c.* 1810. A casting by Stadden, painted by I. N. Greene, Dublin, who owns the model

108 (*above*) Interrogating a prisoner on the Western Front, 1918, with an armoured car in background. The models illustrate the difference between staff and field officers in the First War, which was not solely a matter of uniforms. Britain's and Hill's conversions

109 (*below*) Royal Field Artillery with fifteen pounder guns, c. 1899. Conversions from Britain's in the Author's collection

110 The ultimate in war and models of war. A complex and accurate model of an Atomic Cannon being assembled by an enthusiast of the Royal Army Ordnance Corps

so popular that a quarterly journal is published devoted to its activities.

VEHICLES - Apart from toy guns, the output of vehicles by toy-makers has never kept pace with their horse and foot, although the recent production of plastic kits of motors, guns and fighting vehicles has helped to adjust the balance for Second War collectors. These kits, in two scales, one approximately to standard size, have remarkable accuracy and detail (they often consist of a hundred or more parts all patiently put together), and now include the ultimate in warfare, the atomic cannon [figure 110]. For my collection I have found the plastic kits of vintage motor cars ideal; they are almost in standard scale. A study of old illustrated periodicals of the pre-1914 period shows these vehicles in their military glory. There is General French, cocked hat and all, sitting somewhat selfconsciously in the back of an early Lanchester; there are the Guards on manoeuvres with a Rolls Royce fitted with a machine gun; and in 1914 the German General Staff are pictured advancing towards Liege and Namur in a Mercedes Benz [figures 62

111 (*above*) Early military mechanisation. An ambulance of the First War

112 (*above right*) An armoured car made by Rolls-Royce, used by the Royal Naval Air Service Squadron, 1914

and 108]. For the various unusual and specialist wagons of the horse transport era, I am eternally grateful to the designer of Britain's old 'General Service Wagon' (now out of catalogue), as this vehicle has almost all the basic chassis requirements for a whole range. Old official drawings of airline wagons, gas cylinder or balloon tenders, field ovens and pigeon lofts, show the requirements and this ubiquitous vehicle, cut down, built up, lengthened, re-wheeled and re-shafted, can be adapted to them all [figure 115].

With guns, Britain's has not been quite so obliging to collectors; their field guns have never kept in step with types in service, and there are important gaps in the range for any collector who intends to give artillery the place it deserves. Therefore, some large scale manufacture is necessary, and for this the Britain's pieces are useful for providing wheels, barrels and shields. A fellow collector known to me has obtained brilliant results for thirteen and eighteen pounders and 4.5 inch howitzers by reconstructing the larger Britain's field-guns, but heavier pieces present greater prob-

113 A First War anti-aircraft gun mounted at the rear of an early car, made from Britain's field gun and plastic car-kit by the Author

114 (*above*) A motor-car mounted with a machine-gun, pre-1914 manoeuvres

115 (*above right*) A mobile pigeon-loft of the Royal Engineers, First World War

116 Mounted troops of the Indian Army, 1910-22, including a mounted piper of the 17th Bengal Cavalry. The other castings, by Winkler, are in the Author's collection

lems. The sixty-pounder Long Tom and also the forty-pounder muzzle-loading, elephant-towed equipment of the pre-1914 Indian Army, call for special wheels for which no toy maker's products can be used. Casting the wheels is the only solution. Barrels, recuperator, trails and limbers for these and for a six-inch gun were all made from wood. The early six-inch guns of the First World War had a portable firing platform towed behind when *en passage*, and the whole was drawn by a team of ten heavy draught horses. This equipment symbolises the weight of material which was one of the characteristics of that war, and I was never satisfied until I added a model of one to my collection

117 British heavy artillery in the First World War. An early six-inch gun with firing platform, which was towed by ten horses before the introduction of tractors

[figure 117]. For the horses I found Britain's plough horses suitable for conversion; and for the drivers, I used their state landau postillions.

Governments and armies have not made it easy for the toy-maker, by the bewildering number of changes in types and designs that have been made. Toy-makers naturally like to sell items which have popular appeal and the latest types of equipment in use by armies come in this category. In the early 1950's, realising the need for a good standard size model tank, Britain's took official advice on what would be the most suitable vehicle to copy. As a result they brought out their Centurion. The tools alone for this excellent model cost over £ 4,000.

PLASTIC FIGURES - The plastic soldier, pressed from polysterene or cellulose acetate compounds, has met with a mixed reception from the collector. To my knowledge, the earliest

118 An amateur model-painter at work on renovating one of the Author's own models

pioneer in this field was the late Fred Winkler, a great model soldier enthusiast, always full of ideas (many of which, unfortunately, were impracticable in business). In many ways he was ahead of his time as later developments have shown. In 1946-7 he brought out a range of figures in standard scale, mounted and dismounted. The latter were the better of the two and pressed in component parts (but sold assembled, not as kits). Although there was an acute shortage of lead soldiers at this time, there was a surprisingly strong sales resistance to plastics both as toys and for collectors, and Winkler was obliged to drop his plans for developing the range.

As Garratt so aptly says, at their best plastics 'are brilliant in conception, characterisation, action, colour and

119 The Gloucestershire Regiment in the full dress of about 1900. These are lead figures (Britain's) painted to the correct colours.

general presentation. In details of uniform, chiselling of faces they are superior to their lead counterparts. The worst have nothing to commend them'. The great fear of many collectors is that the plastic soldier will supersede the metal. This is probably inevitable. Manufacturers are already curtailing the range of their lead figures and substituting new lines in plastics. As far as meeting collectors' demands for accuracy goes, these new models are greatly superior in many ways. Britain's original 'Herald' range is now being supplemented by what is called the 'Eyes Right' series, which have spigot heads, nipple arms and various 'attachable' items. Musicians' arms are integrated with beautifully gold-plated instruments, which eliminates one minor difficulty for painters (ie. the tendency of gold mixed with a medium to present a gritty appearance). The 'Eyes Right' series is of contemporary uniforms [figure 124].

Messrs Crescent Toy Co. and Model Toys are two other British firms that are producing high quality standard size plastic soldiers, as well as other figures made traditionally in metal. The American firm of Marx Miniatures is also producing good plastic figures both in the United States

120, 121 (*below*) Pope Pius XII with the *Guardia Nobile* and the Swiss Guards, and (*above*) the standard-bearer and trumpeter. The castings are by Ericksson and Winkler, and the group is now in the Irish Military College Museum

122 The carriage of the Viceroy of India, seen in the previous illustration. It represents the Viceroy, Vicereine, his equipage and servants about 1908. The group was converted from Britain's figures by the Author

and from a factory in England. In Germany, Merten (40 mm) and Elastolin (60 mm.) are the principal producers, but Denmark, Italy, Spain and Eastern European countries too are beginning to make various figures in unbreakable material of one sort or another. Several firms in France are doing the same, one firm specialising in basic torsoes to which a whole series of heads, limbs, uniforms and equipment may be added as desired.

Although a certain amount of collector-resistance is mere conservatism, there are two objections to plastics which have some foundation. Painted with the normal washable or waterproof paint, the finished model tends to crack and so blemish, but experiments with oils will no doubt eliminate this. The second objection is that, to the collector wedded to his soldering iron, hacksaw and files, they call for new methods of conversion. However, French collectors appear to have evolved satisfactory techniques for plastic conversion, and I am indebted to Monsieur J. Girbal and the officers of the *Société des Collectionneurs de Figurines Historiques* for permission to quote the following which may be of help to modellers:

'We recommend for the conversion of figures in either of the plastic materials, the purchase of an *appareil de py-*

123 The 'Battle-axe Company', Royal Artillery, *c.* 1950. Cut-out painted plywood figures, 5½ inches high, by René North

rogramme, which is something like a little soldering iron fitted with a thermometer and which can have different tips.

'When heated to the required temperature, this iron enables the plastic to be moulded rather as moulding sealing wax or modelling clay (do not warm it too much in case the plastic burns and becomes brittle).

'It is in fact easier to work than lead, and the figures can be varied ad infinitum.

'As with metal, matters of detail can be added by moulding with the iron.

'These figures can be 'clothed' as in lead, with a sheet of laminated lead which you inlay, when it is warm, with plastic or more simply with paper which you stick on the plastic.

'Lead details can also be inlaid on the plastic figures, such as sabres, guns and even heads.

'Figurines in cellulose acetate soften when heated. To modify the position of a body, bend an arm or leg, turn a head or even twist a body a little, soak the figure in very warm water for ten to twenty seconds and make the change. It will harden again when it cools.

'Acetate dissolves in acetone. If some pieces of acetate are put in an hermetically sealed vessel with acetone, in a few hours a paste will be obtained. The thickness will depend on the amount of acetone used. This paste is an ideal glue to join the different parts of the figures; it fills any gaps and, smoothing it with the finger, you can get a solid and invisible weld. It can be equally well used as a solder.

'If, as mentioned above, you clothe your figures with paper, soak the paper first in water to avoid little wrinkles. When you have finished, smear the paper with a layer of fairly thin acetate and when it has dried, you will have a figure covered with a plastic-like coat, more resistant to wear and retaining its appearance and rigidity.

'Figures made of Polysterene do not soften in warm water and thus must be worked like lead. Polysterene dissolves in trichlorethlene; it can be stuck together with adhesive used for modelling clay.

'The usual ways to add little details to figures can be employed using fine leather for bridles and buckles for stirrups. Pipe cleaners make excellent feathers and plumes'.

The future therefore appears bright once these and other methods of alteration become known. Plastic figures are admirable in design. Even the chain stores throw up occasional good examples with remarkably fine sculpturing, although there is a tendency for these to be on a large scale.

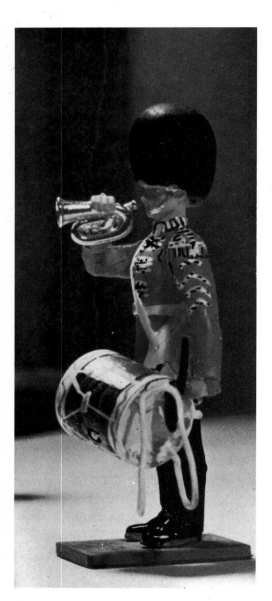

124 A drummer of the Scots Guards about to blow a bugle call. A plastic model from Britain's 'Eyes Right' series. From A. Cleaver's collection

Advice to Collectors

125 Variations from the single unpainted figure, centre left, which the makers, J. Hill & Co, call 'the dismounted General'

TO ANYONE WHO WISHES to become a collector of model soldiers, the following advice may be of assistance. Decide before you acquire many figures what you intend your collection to represent, the period of history, the country or the type of soldiers that interest you. If the desire to collect grows from an existing historical interest, this will already be fairly well defined. You can, of course, have more than one interest but there should be a principal one, and the others secondary. (In my own case, it is the British and Indian Armies, 1890-1916, with the emphasis on the less common types, with Irish, Papal and the bizarre units of all nations as secondary interests). It is a most difficult task for an admirer of soldiers and models in general to discipline himself in collecting.

The books on the hobby listed in a bibliography would

126 Pope John XXIII in his *Sedia Gestatoria*, the chair of state used in papal processions. Author's collection

127 (*opposite*) HM Queen Elizabeth II as Colonel-in-Chief of the Coldstream Guards. A conversion by Captain R. S. Dilley.

be invaluable. Regimental histories, regimental magazines, second-hand illustrated 'period' books, Dress and Equipment Regulations and old drill books will all help to build up a body of knowledge. If you are including equestrian figures in the collection, have at least one good illustrated book on horsemanship. In addition you will find a need for a filing system for picture postcards and cigarette cards of military subjects, (often subjects for collection in their own right but in this case only aids to modelling). Press cuttings and pictures, both old and current, will need scrapbooks for their preservation. These are only part of what Bob Bard appropriately calls source material. There are also museums and exhibitions to be visited, collectors to be written to and their collections to be seen. Attend tattoos and parades when possible. Joining a society can also be a help. I recommend you to join a learned society as well as one for collectors; this keeps a balance between model soldiers as an extension of one's historical interests and models as an end in themselves. Write to all the toy-makers

128 An Allied conversation-piece, North-West Europe, in 1944. The vehicles are plastic, but the soldiers of the American and British armies are Britain's conversions

and custom builders for catalogues and price lists. The former are most long suffering and tolerant of new collectors and the latter's price lists will enable you to budget the building of your collection. When you travel, ascertain beforehand where models and toy soldiers are made, sold or are to be seen, and insist on going to see them. Ask your friends who are going abroad to do likewise on your behalf.

CONVERTING - The work of creating your own figures can begin modestly by repainting commercial figures in the correct colours and gradually extend to the affixing, conversion and casting as you improve your skill [figures 128 and 133]. The best way to learn is by becoming an apprentice to someone who practises it and discover all the secrets and tricks by sitting beside him. Begin by doing all the humble and laborious tasks such as cutting off unwanted parts, rubbing off mould flash, filing down after soldering and making the tea.

To be successful, a conversion needs a good basic figure. If it is already near to what you visualise, the number of saw cuts, the filing down, fillings in, and soldering operations will be reduced. For some requirements there is no near figure: to produce the 1916 steel helmeted lancer, I was compelled to make eight cutting and soldering joints for each figure [figure 133]. All converters keep a stockpile of unused figures and old heads, bodies, legs, weapons, gun parts, odd wheels; never throw anything away. Tools re-

129 A horse-drawn fire-engine of the early 1900s, in the Author's collection, converted from standard basic figures

quired for conversion depend on one's experience and skill as a handyman, but the basic tools must include a small vice, two or three hacksaws, a variety of fine to medium cut files of several shapes, tweezers, pliers, cutters and a lightweight soldering iron. To these in due course you will add your own tools such as an old shoemaker's knife and razor blades.

For soldering hollow castings, the amount of heat to be applied can only be learned by experience. Begin by practising soldering on scrap figures to avoid destroying a masterpiece. Cored solder, as used in radio and electrical work, is the most efficient. With experience comes the realisation that effect can be heightened by adding embellishments; fuse wire for cap lines, bugle cords and aiguillettes; strip lead for belts, slings and other body equipment. (At one time old toothpaste tubes were excellent for the latter, but now that they are made of aluminium, they are no longer suitable). Other items can be added by cold solder, and plastic wood is useful for furnishing items that require a rough

130 A 1916 tank, typical of those used on the Western Front, made by the Author partly from Bristol Board

131 The 16th (Queen's) Lancers, *c.* 1914. Models by Captain R. S. Dilley

look such as guardsmen's bearskin caps. One of my co-modellers achieves wonderful results with this, as will be seen in the Forester's Museum display.

CASTING - Some modellers are not content with the results obtained by conversion and prefer to cast their figures. Casting is not as simple as conversion. To begin with, a master figure is needed for moulding and it can be made by drawing the figure on a piece of wood and roughly cutting it out in full dimension. Make a plaster-of-paris mould of this and after removing the wood figure, cast it in lead. This lead figure can be cut with a sharp knife into a basic nude neuter, preferably astride, with or without a head but almost certainly without arms at this stage. With this key figure more moulding is necessary to produce the number required, the shape of the master figure being altered if malleable enough to give variations in posture. On this nude type of figure, clothing can be built up in the way described by the French society's advice for altering plastics.

An alternative method of casting is to have the moulds made of vulcanised rubber, a specialist technique done by certain firms. These moulds require a very hard, well-

132 Elizabeth II and her officers of state, Some of the figures are part of a limited Coronation edition made by Gammage for Graham Farrish

sculptured master figure; they are only suitable for short 'runs' as the rubber begins to blur. I first saw this technique in use by the late Fred Winkler. His moulds required centrifugal casting, and he used an old hand-operated gramophone to obtain this effect. I served a short apprenticeship to this by winding up the gramophone and regulating the speed. A limited range of very fine figures were produced by this gramophone technique, the 'master' for them being cut by Eriksson [figures 120 and 121].

PAINTING - Little can be usefully said in print which will enable a modeller to paint; there is no sure way to success. One can only begin painting and in time develop individual skills. Here again an association with an experienced model painter is invaluable; by watching him work one quickly learns the need for undercoating, sizes of brushes, mixing of paints, the choice of paints, bases for different models (metal, plastic or wood), and such little techniques as how to hold a model whilst painting it without getting the paint on one's fingers and clothes.

Painting faces is usually a great trial to beginners, and a wooden doll-like effect is hard to avoid. A useful rule is to try the mixture out on your hand first. Remember the shades of tan acquired by soldiers in the tropics, and those special complexions of senior officers of the past with a liking for port. Shadowing and shading of clothes and belts are often aspects of painting that cause trouble; mixing the colour with water and running it out is the method to avoid hard lines. Bullion lace, rank badges, barrel belts and round buttons can be simulated by using a thickened mix of paint with great care, but this is a refinement which usually comes at a later stage.

As Bob Bard has said, 'the model soldier collector is not an antique collector; he is more interested in authenticity than in age'. Neither is he a militarist, as is sometimes believed. Most collectors are first attracted by the glamour of the fighting clothes of the past, which were sometimes so stylish and tight-fitting that it must have been almost impossible to have fought in them. Many great men of letters have taken an interest in the hobby, Goethe, Anatole France, H. G. Wells, R. L. Stevenson, G. K. Chesterton, Lawrence Sterne and, of course, Hans Christian Andersen, whose delightful story of the steadfast tin soldier is famous throughout the world. None of these saw toy soldiers as a threat to peace.

133 An example of a complex conversion. Eight cuts and soldering operations were required to make this 1915 British Lancer

The business of war is now a grim affair, and in this mechanical and nuclear age it is a relief to turn to something which gives a glimpse of the past; of times when individual courage and chivalry were as much a part of war as the picturesque clothes and equipment reproduced in the model soldier.

Farewell the plumed troop and the big wars
That make ambition virtue! O, farewell,
Farewell the neighing steed and the shrill trump,
The spirit-stirring drum, the ear-piercing fife,
The Royal banner and all quality,
Pride, pomp and circumstance of glorious war!
And, O you mortal engines, whose rude throats
The immortal Jove's dread clamours counterfeit,
Farewell! Othello's occupation's gone!